ROUTLEDGE LIBRARY EDITIONS: ADULT EDUCATION

Volume 23

EDUCATIONAL RESPONSES TO ADULT UNEMPLOYMENT

EDUCATIONAL RESPONSES TO ADULT UNEMPLOYMENT

BARBARA SENIOR AND JOHN NAYLOR

LONDON AND NEW YORK

First published in 1987 by Croom Helm Ltd

This edition first published in 2019
by Routledge
2 Park Square, Milton Park, Abingdon, Oxon OX14 4RN

and by Routledge
52 Vanderbilt Avenue, New York, NY 10017

Routledge is an imprint of the Taylor & Francis Group, an informa business

© 1987 Barbara Senior and John Naylor

All rights reserved. No part of this book may be reprinted or reproduced or utilised in any form or by any electronic, mechanical, or other means, now known or hereafter invented, including photocopying and recording, or in any information storage or retrieval system, without permission in writing from the publishers.

Trademark notice: Product or corporate names may be trademarks or registered trademarks, and are used only for identification and explanation without intent to infringe.

British Library Cataloguing in Publication Data
A catalogue record for this book is available from the British Library

ISBN: 978-1-138-32224-0 (Set)
ISBN: 978-0-429-43000-8 (Set) (ebk)
ISBN: 978-1-138-36668-8 (Volume 23) (hbk)
ISBN: 978-1-138-36671-8 (Volume 23) (pbk)
ISBN: 978-0-429-43018-3 (Volume 23) (ebk)

Publisher's Note
The publisher has gone to great lengths to ensure the quality of this reprint but points out that some imperfections in the original copies may be apparent.

Disclaimer
The publisher has made every effort to trace copyright holders and would welcome correspondence from those they have been unable to trace.

Educational Responses to Adult Unemployment

Barbara Senior and John Naylor

CROOM HELM
London • Sydney • Wolfeboro, New Hampshire

© 1987 Barbara Senior and John Naylor
Croom Helm Ltd, Provident House, Burrell Row,
Beckenham, Kent, BR3 1AT

Croom Helm Australia, 44-50 Waterloo Road,
North Ryde, 2113, New South Wales

British Library Cataloguing in Publication Data

Senior, Barbara
    Educational responses to adult employment.
    — (Radical forum on adult education
series)
    1. Unemployed — Education — Great
Britain
    I. Title   II. Naylor, John   III. Series
    374'.941   LC5056.G7
    ISBN 0-7099-3329-0

Croom Helm, 27 South Main Street,
Wolfeboro, New Hampshire 03894-2069, USA

Library of Congress Cataloging-in-Publication Data

Senior, Barbara.
    Educational responses to adult unemployment.

    Includes index.
    1. Continuing education — Great Britain. 2. Unemployed
— Education — Great Britain. 3. Educational innovations —
Great Britain. I. Naylor, John, 1945-
II. Title
LC5256.G7S46   1987   374'.941   86-24106
ISBN 0-7099-3329-0

Printed and bound in Great Britain
by Billing & Sons Limited, Worcester.

CONTENTS

List of Figures
Acknowledgements

Chapter One	Being Unemployed	1
Chapter Two	Unemployment and the Role of Education	27
Chapter Three	Current Educational Responses to Adult Unemployment	40
Chapter Four	The Inadequacy of the Current Situation	69
Chapter Five	Towards a Re-definition of Education for Unemployed Adults	93
Chapter Six	Unemployment Initiatives as Learning Experiences	113
Chapter Seven	Distance Teaching and Self-Paced Learning	131
Chapter Eight	A Model for Distance Learning Provision for Unemployed Adults	146
Chapter Nine	The Future of Work and and the Future of Education	162
INDEX		171

FIGURES

3.1 Typology of Post-initial Education
     Agencies   45

8.1 Centralised Distance Learning
     System   150

8.2 Decentralised Distance Learning
     System   151

ACKNOWLEDGEMENTS

Some four million people inspired the writing of this book. During the research and work on it, we met but a minority, although these were large in number. To these unemployed people we give our thanks for freely contributing their experiences and views.

This book grew out of the development work carried out for the Unemployment Project in the Community Education Department of the Open University. Part of this work involved the many educators, voluntary workers and others who occupy themselves daily in helping those who are unemployed. We gratefully acknowledge the time they gave to assisting our understanding of what education for unemployed adults is and could be.

The book also draws on research, started by the Employment Alternatives Research Group at Liverpool Polytechnic in 1979. Funded by the Joseph Rowntree Memorial Trust, this has collected the ideas and publications of many groups of unemployed people and it is impossible to record all of them. Mention must be made, however, of the members of Tit for Tat at Edinburgh, Manor Employment Project at Sheffield and The Network at Liverpool, all of whom tolerated members of the research team as rather large flies on the wall. Denise Bear, Rita Cordon, Anne Gordon and Karen Holmes were our researchers and their work in included in Chapter six.

Without financial support from the Department of Education and Science and the Manpower Services Commission, the learning materials project on which the discussion in Chapter eight is based, would not have been possible.

Finally, we would like to thank Gerry Senior and Maureen Naylor for their encouragement and practical help with the book's final production.

Barbara Senior
John Naylor

Chapter One

BEING UNEMPLOYED

In the United Kingdom at the present time, there are somewhere between 3 and 4 million unemployed people. The precise number depends on the system of counting used which in turn depends on the way 'being unemployed' is defined. For example, consider the following individuals.

> Julie has recently left school where she studied until she gained two modest GCE 'A' level passes. Whilst still at school she had a weekend job helping in a local grocery store. She hasn't been able to get a full-time job but the grocery store now employs her during the week as well, but still only on a part-time basis. Julie earns about the same as she would get if she were not employed and claiming social security benefit. She wants a full-time job, preferably with some career prospects, and keeps in touch with the Jobcentre in case anything suitable turns up there. Julie likes sewing and spends some of ther time making her own clothes which are judged by her friends to look 'as if they had been bought'.

Mark is nearly 21 years old and has had two jobs since he left college 2 years age. The first lasted 2 months and the second 8 months before he was again made redundant. It is now 7 months since Mark worked. He registered as unemployed, drawing social security benefit during the periods when he did not have a job. He is registering as unemployed now and visits the Jobcentre regularly, as well as watching the adverts in the newspapers in the hope of

Being Unemployed

getting another job. He spends part of most days practising and playing snooker at a local club. He also plays basketball for a local team. Occasionally he helps a couple he knows in their hotel for which he gets money 'in his hand'. He doesn't tell the social security office about this - it only happens in odd weeks for a day or so and it would mean his losing a whole week's benefit.

Jayne was made redundant by her firm after 10 years working for them. She registered immediately as unemployed and began planning the setting up of her own business. She found out that, provided she was registered unemployed at the time of application, she was eligible to be considered for a place on a government sponsored scheme to help new businesses, which guarantees weekly payments during the first year of trading. Jayne has contacts who will give her business now. However, she has been advised by the Jobcentre that, even though this presently available work would fall far short of supporting herself and her mother, she cannot take it unless she wants to forego her unemployed status and benefit and therefore her eligibility for the scheme. She has also been informed that it will be at least 3 months before she can get on to the scheme, if she is accepted. Jayne has decided that she cannot chance becoming self-employed without the guaranteed payments to fall back on in case of lack of trade. She has, therefore, had to let the present chances of business go, and perhaps jeopardise these contacts for the future, in the hope that she will get a place on the scheme in 3 months time. She is allowed to make all the administrative preparations for self-employment including advertising and marketing. She is therefore working at getting an office arranged, seeing the bank manager and accountant, enquiring about stationery and telephone as well as preparing prospectuses and advertising material. This means that she is not able to spend as many Sundays away walking and rock climbing as she used to when she worked for her old firm.

Being Unemployed

Christine is married with two children aged 13 and 14. She has not worked since the children were born. She has, however, taken a great deal of interest in the parent-teachers association at the children's school, serving on the committee and chairing it for 3 years. Some years ago she helped for a while at her local Citizens Advice Bureau and is often now approached by neighbours and friends for advice and help over a wide range of issues. She has, in addition, become well known among her children's friends for her ability to 'do mathematics' and spends many an hour with one or another sorting out their frequent confusions with their school homework. Christine used, before the birth of her children, to work as a wages clerk and now that her children are approaching independence wants to take up full-time employment again, although she would consider a part-time job or sharing a full-time job with someone else. Although she studies the situations vacant in the local newspaper, she hardly ever finds anything she feels she has the skills and ability to do. She has now enrolled at her local college for a course in computing, this being the sort of thing everyone is saying is needed now and in the future.

Brian is married with three children aged 7 to 14 years. He lives in Liverpool and has not had a job now for just over 3 years. Many of Brian's neighbours are also unemployed. His wife used to have a part-time job, but gave it up because the majority of her earnings were offset by reductions in the benefit her husband received. Brian has given up any active search for jobs. He stays at home much of the time, occasionally going to the Jobcentre with perhaps one night out per week. He has thought of moving to another part of the country but can't contemplate leaving other parts of his family who live nearby (the childen's grandmother sometimes 'treats' them), even if he could get another council house somewhere else.

These descriptions of individuals are based on real live people who all think of themselves as

Being Unemployed

unemployed. Only Mark, Jayne and Brian, however, are counted as unemployed by the Department of Employment (because they claim benefits) and so only they appear in the official unemployment statistics. Even though Mark has not had a job for 7 months, he is still not classified as long-term unemployed, he would need to have been unemployed for at least 12 months before he becomes one of the million or more registered in this category.

It is not difficult to imagine the variety of attitudes displayed towards these five people by others in terms of whether or not they are unemployed. Much depends on the meanings put by people upon the concept of unemployment, what it is and how it came about. To understand more fully what unemployment and being unemployed means it is necessary to consider what having a job means, that is being employed, as well as the broader concept of work.

Consider firstly the word 'work'. What connotations does it have for most people? A common saying is 'I only work for the money', or someone might say, 'I dug the whole of my garden over at the weekend and it was really hard work'. Most people know of someone who does 'voluntary' work, maybe in a Citizens Advice Bureau, for which they are carefully trained by the organisation, or helping with church and school social activities which have no formal acceptance procedures nor require any special knowledge and abilities. A person might work to repair her neighbour's car as a form of community good will.

There is a degree of confusion regarding the way the concept of work is used, its commonly accepted meaning has changed over time. David Macarov echoes this confusion when he says, 'As is true of many other important concepts, it is difficult to arrive at a generally accepted, exclusive, inclusive definition of work'.[1] There have, even so, been attempts to do just this for example, Robin Guthrie in the first newsletter of Work & Society wrote,

> Work is a strong word. It is the kind of noise you make as you drive the spade into a lump of clay, or heave a bale to the top of the rick: one of the grunts of primitive man. It comes to us across the millenia from Indo-European roots through the Greek 'ergon' which gives us also

Being Unemployed

> the term 'erg': a unit of energy. That is the secret of the word: 'work' entails effort. Its opposite is rest.[2]

Implied in this description of work is the idea that work equals manual work. There is the implication of 'honest toil' and men's work. This quotation illustrates the meaning of work in its historic sense attached to a value system which focuses on survival and security needs, what Yankelovich et al[3] call the values of sustenance.

This particular value system prevailed prior to the industrial revolution when most work in and outside the home contributed directly to satisfying basic survival needs of food, clothing, shelter and some security in case of illness and for old age. Although the quotation with its stress on hard physical labour implies men's work, historically men and women contributed interdependently to family survival. Work in these terms is structured activity[4] which may or may not be enjoyable, indeed Macarov says, 'At no time during this period,... does work seem to have been viewed as pleasant, ennobling, or moral'. Survival meant work and work meant survival.

Nowadays people tend to expect at least some enjoyment out of working, even so it is still not considered a necessary condition.

> In general terms 'work' may be defined as an activity beyond enjoyment of the activity itself... Work can vary from momentary exertion through to efforts sustained over a period of time. Sustained activity almost always takes place within a network of social roles and institutions.[5]

Note the reference to social roles and institutions allows the inclusions in this definition, of activities such as housework, child and relative care, voluntary work and educational study.

In contrast Guthrie, following on from his illustration of work, goes on in his article to suggest that modern definitions are different from the one he quotes, work now meaning 'earning a living' the opposite of which, he suggests, is leisure. Certainly books and reports like 'World Out of Work' and 'Growing Up Without Work' have an underlying assumption that work means paid work or,

Being Unemployed

as the House of Lords Select Committee on Unemployment[6] defines it, employment.
Employment then is essentially a concept which has developed with the new forms of work associated with the industrial revolution.

> Employment occurs when the individual receives economic reward for his/her labours. It involves the performance of activities which have a market value... Essentially employment is the <u>relationship</u> between the employee and the <u>employer</u> - a relationship based on exchange.[7]

Peter Warr in his discussion from which the above definition of work is taken, describes paid work as 'sustained activity which involves payment'.[8] So work as employment no longer attaches to a value system based solely on sustenance. It has become the norm that satisfaction of sustenance, survival and security needs is gained through the purchasing power of money earned within an employment relationship, and, because industrialised societies are able to produce an abundance of wealth as well as supporting a welfare system for those who are unable to work in employment 'the stage is set for a major shift in values... On a massive scale individuals are now free to pursue personal needs beyond survival and basic security'.[9]

So, as has happened in the United Kingdom when satisfaction of sustenance needs are taken for granted, the prevailing system becomes one of material success, based on values which Yankelovich et al describe as relating primarily to requirements for growing prosperity, for order, ambition and efficiency.

> These values have their roots in industrial society in what Max Weber has called Instrumental Rationality. The key words are 'standard of living' and 'productivity' and values centre on being part of the productive process and on the creation of capital.[10]

The post war period in this country was one where the values of material success could be satisfied for most people through employment.
It is clear that having a job, being employed, is only one form of work in spite of the propensity

Being Unemployed

nowadays to speak of work as if it only meant a job. However, paid work is for most people their only means of enhancing their material well-being and people have, therefore, come to regard having a job as extremely important and in most cases a necessity. Being employed is regarded as an entitlement rather than a favour. Work as employment is clearly related to the concept of unemployment; but what about work in the sense of being **any** structured activity beyond enjoyment of the activity itself?

Charles Handy[11] has usefully described employment and work as taking place within three economies. He begins by defining economy as a set of activities which in some way or other add value to the world. He divides 'the economy' into three; the market, redistribution and informal economies.

The market economy 'consists of all businesses whose job it is to make things or to provide services for money to those who want them',[12] it consists of paid work. The businesses may be run by private enterprise or be publicly owned. People pay for the products or services provided by these businesses and those who work in them are in a situation of being employed. The businesses in the market economy earn foreign exchange to pay for imports from other countries. Taxes are paid on business profits, but in larger amounts through employees' income tax and national insurance as well as from VAT on goods and services sold.

The second economy is the redistribution economy, so called because it redistributes the money collected from the market economy to services like schools, hospitals, the police and welfare benefit services; services for which recipients do not pay. Like the market economy, however, the people working in the redistribution economy are employed and pay taxes. So, even though money could be saved by reducing the size of the redistribution economy, the taxes of people working in it would be lost and the purchasing power of institutions like the National Health Service (which increases income to the market economy which in turn provides money for the redistribution economy) would also be reduced. Of the five people introduced at the beginning of the chapter, only Julie does any work in these two 'formal' economies.

The third economy, the informal economy, which Handy refers to as the 'uncounted economy', has three parts; the black economy, the household economy and the voluntary economy.

> In the informal economy, we make things, grow things, cook things, wash things and repair things for ourselves, and for others, but because we usually charge no money for them they don't get counted or taxed, or included in the calculations of national wealth.[13]

Stuart Henry[14] echoes this definition of the informal economy but adds that activities within this context are likely to be part-time rather than full-time.

Henry discusses a number of ways of subdividing the informal economy but essentially they differ very little from Handy's. Thus the black (Handy) or irregular (Henry) economy is 'work which really belongs to the market economy but because no-one declares it, it does not get counted (or taxed)'.[15] Implicit in this description is Henry's reference to money as the medium of exchange. The extent of activity in the black economy is difficult to measure but may be as 'large as seven per cent of the two formal economies combined',[16] or even larger (16%).[17]

The other two types of informal economy are the household ('production, not for money, by members of a household and predominantly for members of a household, of goods and services for which approximate substitutes might otherwise be purchased for money'[18]) and voluntary or communal ('production, not for money or barter, by an individual or group, of a commodity that might otherwise be purchasable and of which the producers are not principal consumers'[19]). Handy maintains that some five million people do voluntary unpaid work involving something like two hundred thousand voluntary organisations. He states further that more than half the whole population are in the informal economy. Indeed in a talk given as part of a symposium on the Future of Work, Handy referred to fifty per cent of the people of working age not being in jobs.

Clearly these people include the 3 million 'official' unemployed.[20] It is debatable, however, whether these and other unemployed people are involved in any significant way in work outside the formal economies. Of the people described earlier,

Being Unemployed

Julie might be judged to work in the household economy by making her own clothes; Christine clearly does work in the household and voluntary economies; David has some small involvement in the black economy; but neither Jayne nor Brian could be said to take any significant part in the informal economy, except for a minority involvement in housework.

What is clear is that people who consider themselves and are considered by others to be unemployed can, in theory, still work, that is participate in structured activity and gain some satisfaction, even though paid work may not be available to them. The reasons that, according to a number of sources[21] they do not, enables a deeper understanding of what employment and being unemployed means.

UNEMPLOYMENT

If employment is defined as paid work then unemployment is the absence of paid work. However, many people who do not do paid work, that is do not have a job, would not consider themselves nor be thought of by others as being unemployed. If, as Handy says, only half the people of working age are in jobs, then a substantial number of those not in jobs can be judged to be so out of choice. These include women and men who choose to be involved for much of their time in housekeeping and childcare and others who have retired from jobs before the designated 'official' time, but who do not, all the same, wish to take other jobs. There are of course other examples of people who would not want paid work.

The majority of all these individuals have some kind of unearned income (housekeeping allowances, pensions, welfare benefits) or have their basic needs paid for by others. They almost certainly do substantial amounts of work in the household and voluntary economies. So, who can be classed as unemployed, and do these people differ in their characteristics and activities from those who do not do paid work by choice?

The 1984 HMSO publication from the Central Statistics Office entitled 'Social Trends', includes the unemployed (along with employees, the self-employed and members of HM Forces) within the

Being Unemployed

category of people labelled 'economically active'. It refers to the unemployed as 'all those who are out of a job and looking for work', a definition which goes beyond those who are able to claim welfare benefits. This definition implies that the unemployed are 'out of work', not by choice but because they have not managed to find a job. Unemployment for these people is not something they have chosen. It has, as it were, chosen them. It has been forced upon them.

Now, it would appear that the last thing that 'those who are out of a job and looking for work' are is 'economically active', particularly those who claim benefit through Unemployment Benefit Offices. The earnings rules are such that part-time or casual earnings of anything more than a token amount affect directly the benefit entitlement.[22] There is no incentive whatsoever to 'top up' benefit entitlements either on the part of the unemployed themselves or their dependents. In Jonathan Bradshaw's words, 'There is very little labour participation by people receiving social security'.[23] Neither do spouses earn to top up the family income, reasons being that for claimants receiving unemployment benefit,

> ... if their spouse earns more than the dependent adult's allowance (£16.70) the claimant loses the whole of this. On supplementary benefit all the earnings of the claimant and spouse over £4.00 each is deducted from benefit.[24]

Reference to DHSS Social Security Statistics of 1983 and a forthcoming report of the DHSS cohort study of unemployed men concludes that 'the wives of unemployed men are less likely to be employed than other wives'.[25] So unemployment means having no job when one is wanted, but, for men in particular, it also means having little hope of extra family income from their wives' earnings unless these are derived from other than part-time and low paid jobs, which are frequently the norm.

A possibility exists, of course, that whilst unemployed people may not be active in the formal economy, they are putting their energies into the informal economy; they are working even though they may not be legitimately employed. The evidence for this is far from convincing.

Being Unemployed

Consider firstly, the black part of the informal economy. As previously mentioned there are a variety of estimates of participation in the black economy. Michael O'Higgins in a survey of research concerning what he terms the 'hidden' economy and based on his own investigations concludes that any assumption of rapid growth in the hidden economy is unproven. However, even if the black economy is not growing significantly and regardless of the size of it, one can still speculate on a possible connection between it and informal economic activities amongst the unemployed.

Wallace refers to arguments that maintain that the unemployed have the most incentive to increase their income via the black economy. After surveying the evidence, and on the basis of her own research Wallace concludes, '...there is no concrete evidence that it is the unemployed who are most likely to be engaged in the black economy'.[26] The reasons are supported directly by Henry,[27] Pahl,[28] and Jahoda[29] as well as indirectly by findings (to be discussed later) regarding the psychological effects of unemployment. These centre mainly on the facts that unemployed people have neither the skills, nor the finance for anything other than occasional casual work. Nor does their depressed, despondent and passive state provide the motivation to face the considerable risks involved. In addition,

> ...those regions and local areas with the highest levels of unemployment are frequently those with the poorest social infrastructure and the very fact of high unemployment means relative poverty and restricted markets for black economy products and services.[30]

The overall conclusion is that unemployment has not got a great deal to do with the black economy. It is the employed who are much more likely to be 'moonlighting', that is having second jobs the income from which is not part of their declared earnings.

A consideration of the other sectors of the informal economy - the household and voluntary - shows a similar picture. There have been several pieces of research which have documented how unemployed people spend their time. Bunker and Dewberry's[31] research concerned 192 people from 8 different locations in England, equal numbers of men

Being Unemployed

and women aged 16 to unspecified ages over 46. Trew and Kilpatrick[32] collected time diaries from 150 men aged 25 to 45 years in Belfast and compared them with similar research by Miles involving 124 men of similar age in Brighton.

All these studies found that unemployed people spend far more time in the home than when they were employed and when compared with other employed people. According to Bunker and Dewberry this is not wholly due to lack of money. Their mixed sample of men and women showed changes from out-of-home to home-based activities with significantly more television watching, housework and reading, and a marked reduction in going out for entertainment, playing sport, community and social activities.

Trew and Kilpatrick found that their Belfast sample of men spend about two thirds of their waking time in the home, the largest proportion of this time (average 5.2 hours per day) being spent in what they termed 'passive leisure', that is television, radio, reading, chat, music and just sitting. The largest proportion was in television watching. Some 3 hours a day on average was spent on domestic chores and child care. Social life occupied only one and a half hours on average each day with less for sport and active leisure and hardly any on work, civic and religious activities. Only three respondents spent any time at all on voluntary work, although some of the DIY activities (44 minutes per day), included in the domestic chores categories, may have been for other people. Only minor differences in time use were reported by Miles'[33] sample of Brighton men.

It is clear from this research that unemployed people are not spending their time in the voluntary economy, a conclusion supported by research based on a sample of 1,043 men and women. Thus:

> Only 16 per cent of unemployed people aged 16 or over who were interviewed in the survey in 1981 said they had done some form of voluntary work in the 12 months before the interview, a lower proportion than that for other economic activity groups.[34]

Clearly unemployed people do not form any significant proportion of the 5 million voluntary unpaid workers mentioned by Handy.[35] Neither are they throwing themselves wholeheartedly into

Being Unemployed

domestic and DIY activities although the former certainly increased. Pahl's comments regarding his study of all forms of work in 730 households in the Isle of Sheppey, Kent provide a useful summary statement.

> The results were striking and unequivocal: most work done outside employment is done by members of households for themselves or, to a lesser extent, for relatives. They work with their own tools in their own time **but only if they are in employment.** (Pahl's emphasis)... The Sheppey survey demonstrated unequivocally that employment status is the key to participation in **all** forms of work. There is **not** a trade off between time and money as some have asserted and the part-time female workers are typically in households which already have a number of earners.[36]

At the risk of over statement, it is worthwhile in this context to quote Pahl's final statement, which although based on the Kent study, is entirely in line with the other research in this area.

> ... the growth of new, part-time employment in areas of high unemployment is unlikely to add to the benefit of households whose head is not already in employment. The most rapidly growing type of employment does not necessarily help those households in which there are no earners and who most want work. Furthermore, members of these households are also the least likely to be engaged in other kinds of informal work.[37]

In a phrase, unemployment means being forced out of employment and being denied paid work. In addition, as has been shown, it also means being without work in its wider sense. Neither do unemployed people enjoy substantial leisure. Guthrie said that the opposite of work is rest and the opposite of employment is leisure. Leisure is the counterpart of work. Rest and leisure only have meaning, therefore, in the presence of work and employment. Warr sums this up when he says, 'Leisure (is) the opportunity **not** to work.'[38] However, unemployment is certainly not the 'opportunity' not to work. Unemployment means no job and no work and little leisure (in any active sense). The

Being Unemployed

consequences of this for those who experience it are far reaching.

BEING UNEMPLOYED

For the individual who is unemployed, being unemployed means being denied access to the formal economy and having no motivation nor encouragement to work. The most obvious effect of this is the financial one and the lack of status of an employed person, in spite of the fact that, 'the large majority of people out of work nowadays are clearly employable and clearly want a job.'[39] Mention has already been made of the value system prevailing since the industrial revolution, one concerned with material success.

Being unemployed means having reduced opportunity to acquire the symbols of material success. Most unemployed people live on reduced incomes relative to previous earnings[40] or compared to those with jobs. Robert Taylor,[41] calculated a drop of 46 per cent and Warr[42] refers to studies of unemployed working class men which suggest that two thirds of them had only half or less income than when employed. Even those whose employment conditions have included certain 'insurances' or 'hedges' to alleviate the effect of redundancy, eventually have to lower their own and their dependents' standards of living. Reduced income restricts the opportunity to participate in a wide variety of leisure and other activities. Common sense suggests that any activities which incur direct (subscriptions, entrance fees, etc.) and indirect (travelling, dress) costs will, of necessity, be constrained.

In addition to financial penalties, unemployment brings with it a variety of physical, psychological and social consequences. Certain traditional values are associated with job holding:- male self-esteem, being a 'good provider' for the family, enhancing material well-being, respectability, identity and achievement.[43] However, having a paid job is also important for newer cultural values; enhancing one's economic and psychological independence (particularly for women and younger people), self-fulfilment, empowerment, effectiveness and autonomy, all part of what might be called the values of expressivism.[44] So, being

Being Unemployed

unemployed may be expected to be a depressing and demoralising experience. In a culture dominated by the work ethic, Adrian Sinfield summarises well the way unemployed people are regarded. He says;

> The very fact that employment is established for those without private means as the normal and legitimate way of life, and of supporting oneself and any family, places those who are out of work in a suspect and ambiguous, if not deviant position.[45]

A number of comprehensive surveys of the now substantial research and literature relating to the psychological and social impact of unemployment have been made.[46] The following conclusions draw on these unless otherwise stated.

Physical Health

There is extensive evidence of a statistically significant connection between unemployment and ill-health, but there is some debate about the direction and strength of the causal link.[47] However, as unemployment increases, the proportion of people whose health leads to them becoming unemployed should decrease. In practice, the opposite trend has occurred which would appear to point to unemployment itself contributing to increased ill-health. The House of Lords Committee on Unemployment[48] considered the evidence relating to relationships between unemployment and health, and although recognising that the direction of causation is not confirmed, came to a similar conclusion to that of Tyrrell and Shanks that 'the balance of the evidence, and the more intuitive perspective most certainly do not serve to refute the hypothesis of a causal link running from unemployment to bad health'.[49] Care should be taken, however, to note that the long-term unemployed are more likely to include working class men than other groups and these are more prone to ill-health than the general population of working age.

There are strong indications that unemployment is a factor in the reversal of the 1960's downward trend in the suicide rate. Studies also show that areas with high unemployment have a higher than normal mortality rate both among people of working age and among young children aged under 4 years. Warr,[50] in his review of research concerning the

Being Unemployed

economic recession and mental health, quite rightly cautions against assuming that unemployment leads to physical ill-health. However, it seems unlikely that, other than in a few cases, unemployment leads to beneficial changes in people's physical health. The reverse is much more likely.

Psychological Consequences

Jimmy Barnes, an unemployed fitter, writing about the development and activities of unemployment centres, says, 'Unemployment does things to people's minds, it makes an active life very difficult.'[51] Work & Society held a 'Talkabout' in West Yorkshire about the future of work when they got a range of community, grass-roots and county-level groups to discuss probems of unemployment. The report[52] of this month-long activity involving 17 groups and 4 public meetings includes a discussion of the meanings given to being employed and being unemployed. Three broad sets of meanings came up over and over again. These were:

employment=respect; unemployment=worthlessness
employment=money; unemployment=poverty
employment=order; unemployment=anarchy

Jimmy Barnes' observation is reflected in some of the comments made by the people involved, particularly regarding unemployment and worthlessness. The following are some examples:

...Then, because of redundancies, you feel as if your feet have been kicked away from under you ... I was totally disorientated, really disillusioned, and I feel very bitter.

...And because I'm nearly fifty years old, nobody wants to know you.

I've known friends who've been made redundant and they've been virtually on the point of a nervous breakdown - because they haven't the interests to occupy them ... They just sit there, just ... just vegetating.

It's the destruction of your whole being, your raison d'etre.

Being Unemployed

> The school leaver needs a job to feel independent. It's partly the money, but it is not just that: it's the relationship to family and the sense of being in charge of one's life.
>
> Those who are unemployed feel left out ... They feel they have no place in society.
>
> A man's not a real man unless he has a job.
>
> I wouldn't respect my father if he didn't go out to work and come home with a wage.
>
> There's a stigma from being on the dole; you're labelled as a scrounger.

These comments, given in informal discussions, echo much of the carefully controlled research on this aspect of unemployment.

In 1979, Marie Jahoda[53] wrote that little was known of the effects of unemployment in the 1970s. Since then, there has accumulated a great deal of evidence indicating that being unemployed is a demoralising and stigmatising experience affecting people's mental well-being in many ways. Being unemployed is almost always described in terms of what is lost as a result of not having paid work. So both Jahoda and Warr[54] have described the functions which work fulfils for people and which are, for the most part lost when an individual becomes unemployed. Thus, apart from pay and conditions which Jahoda calls the manifest functions of employment, there are certain latent functions which paid work fulfils. These are, in Jahoda's words, firstly that employment **imposes a time structure** on the working day; secondly, employment implies **regularly shared experiences and contacts** with people ouside the nuclear family; thirdly, employment **links an individual to goals and purposes** which transcends his/her own; fourthly, employment defines aspects of **personal status and identity**; fifthly, employment **enforces** activity. Warr adds a number of other features of unemployment, namely reduced **decision latitude**, that is the reduction in the range of realistic options concerning lifestyle; reduction in **skill use and development**; an increase in **psychologically threatening activities**, that is facing repeated job rejections and being considered a second class citizen amongst others; and

Being Unemployed

insecurity about the future, possible loss of self-respect, unemployability, and insoluble money problems. Being unemployed has clearly got little positive potential.

It is important, however, amongst this catalogue of despair not to assume that all unemployed people are in a permanent state of desperation verging on mental breakdown. As with the general population unemployed individuals vary a good deal one from another and given some basic, though perhaps inadequate, welfare provision individuals will react to having no job in a variety of ways. Some may even welcome the release from jobs which are essentially boring, uninteresting or dangerous. Having said this, it is unusual to find unemployed people on the whole enjoying the material and psychological rewards that being employed brings.

This is particularly so with the greater incidence of long-term unemployment (now over 1 million unemployed for over a year) and experience by others of repeated job loss. On the basis of extensive cross-sectional and longitudinal research, Warr reports that, 'Moving from paid work to unemployment yields an overall very significant reduction in psychological well-being'.[55] Changes occurring were increased anxiety, depression, insomnia, irritability, lack of confidence, listlessness, inability to concentrate and general nervousness. However, the severity of the psychological consequences is mediated by a number of factors.

Firstly, the degree of attachment to paid employment is positively associated with the degree of psychological distress during unemployment. Thus if employment or occupation is the main focus for a person's identity, the impact of job loss is increased. Consequently, men, single women and principal earner women are most likely to suffer psychological distress, and this is generally the case. Married women and mothers are said to be less affected perhaps because of their having access to an alternative identity focus in the role of housewife.

In fact, the effects of unemployment on women are complex and have not been investigated to anything like the same extent as have the effects on men. There is some evidence that differential effects occur according to class which is linked to home environment. Thus for women (likely to be

Being Unemployed

working class) whose home environment is impoverished and stressful, employment is more of a means of escape and improvement than for middle class women.[56]

Another problem is that the extent of female unemployment is difficult to judge. Many women are not eligible for benefits and therefore do not appear in the statistics or in the dole queues. For instance, in 1981, 41 per cent of married women who, according to the Labour Force Survey[57] declared themselves as unemployed were not included in the official statistics compared to 25 per cent of non-married women and 10 per cent of men. In addition to both registered and non-registered unemployed women, there are probably many more who have been discouraged from looking for jobs, but who would do so in an improved economic climate, than there are those who want full-time jobs but who can only get part-time marginal employment. The effects of the economic recession on these women is difficult to judge. What is indisputable is that, in periods of high unemployment, it is women in the role of housekeepers and managers of family finances who have much of the burden to bear.

Variations in degree of psychological distress can also be found between different age groups, distress being lower for the younger (under 25 years) and older (over 55 years) unemployed. For the latter group, there is the possibility of taking on the identity of those approaching retirement, an accepted social role. However, it is this group which is more vulnerable to longer terms of unemployment, who have little chance of getting another job following redundancy.

As far as the young are concerned, various explanations for their seeming buoyancy in the face of decreasing job opportunities have been put forward. The most prevalent is that, in a similar way to women and older men, the young can adopt an alternative role - child/student/trainee. In addition, if they have never had a stable job, they have not become socialised into the work and career role and so do not experience the same sense of loss as those in their middle years. It is possible that, as many young people still live in their parents' homes, they may have some financial and other kinds of support. The under 20s in particular carry forward from school a network of friends and activities. The social stigma of unemployment may

Being Unemployed

not be as great for them. It is the case that most of the attention being paid to the unemployed since the late 1970s has been focused on the young, which may have had the effect of making them feel that at least something was being attempted to alleviate their situation. On the other hand, there have been signs of social unrest among the young which give some indication of a sense of alienation.[58]

There is a number of descriptions of the way individuals react to being unemployed as the length of time without a job increases. Typical are the phase theories of unemployment, which suggest a number of different stages that unemployed people pass through. The initial response to job loss can be dramatic, a feeling that the bottom of one's world has dropped out. Paradoxically, this is followed by a denial of what is taking place. The individual looks upon him or herself as having the same occupational identity. Often this period is seen as an opportunity to have a holiday, do odd jobs about the house and think about more leisure activities. This state of optimism generally lasts only a short time and tends to be followed by an intermediate stage when, after all the jobs about the house have been done, savings are exhausted and job applications are being rejected, the individual begins to take on the identity and standard of living of an unemployed person. This is a period of depression, boredom, having a sense of futility and feeling under-valued. This is when an increase in 'passive' leisure type activities occurs - staying longer in bed, watching television and lazing about.

The intermediate stage is followed by a third one of settling down to unemployment. 'Anxiety, struggle and hope all decline and the individual and his family adjust to the standard and lifestyle implied by living off benefit and being out of work.'[59] As this adjustment happens, deterioration of psychological well-being ceases, though still remaining low, and resignation sets in. There are some differences in the times at which changes from one phase to another are said to occur. Hill[60] suggests times of up to two months; between two and nine months; and after nine months for the three phases. Warr and Jackson[61] report research which suggests shorter periods but continues to support the phase theory, at least in respect of unemployed semi-skilled and unskilled men. Deterioration of general and psychological health continues to increase until a levelling off time at about 6 months of continuous unemployment. The exceptions to this trend are the under 20s and those over 59.

It would appear that the group of unemployed people most at risk, as far as the psychological impact of unemployment is concerned, is that which includes middle aged men and main wage-earning women who have been unemployed for some time. If they are additionally from the lower socio-economic classes, then lower earnings before unemployment (which clearly affects their financial state after job loss), coupled with the likelihood of having fewer coping strategies, increase their vulnerability.

The danger in this conclusion is that other groups such as unemployed and underemployed married women, middle class executives and those approaching retirement age tend to be overlooked. Also, in the case of women and older people there may be some underlying assumptions that they can be cancelled out of the labour market. As far as the young unemployed are concerned, these are presently being systematically encouraged to take on a student/trainee role which, although intended to lead to employment, quite often does not. This has subsequent negative consequences for the development of adult roles and identities. Just what the consequences of this retardation of entry into 'adult working life' will be is a matter for speculation.

Home and Family
Unemployment affects more people than those who are directly unemployed. It affects other individuals in their families and living conditions generally.[62] For instance there is good evidence that homelessness occurs as a direct result of unemployment. Young people leave the parental home in search of employment and, if a job is not found quickly, will become homeless. Some unemployed people lose their homes because they fail to pay their rent or mortgage payments. A vicious circle is set up whereby once homeless, the likelihood of repeated spells of unemployment increases dramatically.

Unemployment also pervades family life. Hakim reports:

> All studies of the unemployed which enquire into the impact of family relationships report

> an increase in friction, stress and tension between spouses, and to a lesser extent between parents and children.[63]

Divorce appears to be much more frequent among couples experiencing spells of unemployment. Hakim comments on the mean total duration of spells of unemployment among divorcing couples being double that for stable marriages.[64] So, relatively high divorce and separation rates plus some increase in death rates among the unemployed can be expected to lead to an increase in the numbers of one-parent families.

Parental unemployment can affect children's health, behaviour and educational attainment. The 1980 survey of 8000 unemployed people carried out by the Policy Studies Institute showed,

> Four types of problem occured quite frequently in the families of unemployed men, but were rarely reported in families where the mother was unemployed: truancy problems, missing school due to health problems, reading problems, and referrals to an educational psychologist.[65]

This conculsion is supported in essence by data from the National Children's Bureau cohort study, beginning in 1958, as well as others.

THE WIDER EFFECT

Being unemployed is clearly a problem from the point of view of the individual and his or her family. Its effects, however, spread even further. The fear of unemployment affects those in jobs through feelings of insecurity of employment and career stagnation. Opportunities grow fewer and people 'put up' with things that they are unable to change.

The 'ripple effect' does not stop here, though. Sinfield[66] points out the economic costs of wasted labour and lost production, but as importantly, the slowing down and even reversal of the achievement of desirable societal goals, such as objectives for health, education and living environments, as well as increasing equality of job opportunities and reducing discrimination.

Being Unemployed

In conclusion, being unemployed appears to be a fairly miserable experience for those individuals directly affected. It also has indirect negative consequences for others and its effects spread through to the overall fabric of society itself. The 'problem' of unemployment can thus be defined in many ways. 'Solutions' will not be easily come by and may require a radical new conceptualisation of the meanings of work, employment and unemployment. The future of work and society is by no means clear.

What is clear is that, if there is a belief that education can be a means to increase personal growth and assets, to build more abilities and empower people in their actions, then in this situation there is a role for education to play. This is particularly true for those who are unemployed.

NOTES

1. David Macarov, <u>Work and Welfare: The Unholy Alliance</u>, Sage Publications, London, (1980), p.19
2. Robin Guthrie, 'What Do We Mean By Work', <u>Work and Society Newsletter No.1.</u>(1983)
3. Daniel Yankelovich et al, <u>Work and Human Values: An International Report on Jobs in the 1980's and 1990's</u>, Aspen Institute for Humanistic Studies, (1983)
4. Op. cit., p.21
5. Peter Warr, 'Work, Jobs and Unemployment', <u>Bulletin of the British Psychological Society 36</u>, (1983), pp.305-311
6. H.M.S.O., <u>Report from the Select Committee of the House of Lords on Unemployment</u>, 1982
7. Jean Hartley, 'Psychological Approaches to Unemployment', <u>Bulletin of the British Psychological Society, 33</u>, (1980), pp.412-414
8. Warr, op. cit.
9. Yankelovich, op. cit., p.47
10. Ibid., p.47
11. Charles Handy, <u>Taking Stock: Being Fifty in the Eighties,</u> British Broadcasting Corporation, London, (1983)
12. Ibid., p.21
13. Ibid., p.22
14. Stuart Henry, 'The Working Unemployed: Perspectives on the Informal Economy and

Unemployment', *The Sociological Review, New Series,* (August 1982), pp.460-477

15. Handy, op. cit., p.23
16. Ibid., p.23
17. Claire Wallace, writing in the *Work and Society Newsletter No.3* (January 1984), discusses the possible participation rates of people in the black economy. She refers to estimates of 16% of Gross National Product by Ken Matthews at the University of Liverpool
18. Henry, op. cit., p.461
19. Ibid., p.461
20. There were 3 million unemployed (excluding school leavers) in January 1984, according to the Central Statistical Office publication of Monthly Digest of Statistics, No.458, February 1984. The figure of 3 million includes only those people who claim benefit at Unemployment Benefit Offices
21. The low participation rates of unemployed people in the informal economy is referred to in the following discussion of 'unemployment'
22. Jonathan Bradshaw, 'Disincentives to Working in the Benefit System', *Work and Society Newsletter, No.4*, (April 1984)
23. Ibid., p.3
24. Ibid.
25. *Social Trends 1984* (HMSO) has its Social Groups chapter devoted to the unemployed. Table 13.5 shows that in 1982, 42 per cent of employed male heads of households had wives who also were employed compared to 18 per cent of unemployed male heads of households
26. Wallace, op. cit., p.7
27. Henry, op. cit.
28. Ray Pahl, 'Deindustrialisation and Social Polarisation', *Work and Society Newsletter No.4*. (April 1984)
29. Marie Jahoda, 'The Impact of Unemployment in the 1930s and the 1970s, *Bulletin of The British Psychological Society, 32*, (1979), pp.309-314
30. Henry, op, cit., p.467
31. Nigel Bunker and Chris Dewberry, *Unemployment Behind Closed Doors*, Mimeograph, (1982)
32. Karen Trew and Rosemary Kilpatrick, *The Daily Life of the Unemployed*, Department of Psychology, Queens University, Belfast, (1984)
33. Ian Miles, *Adaptation to Unemployment*, Mimeo, Science Policy Research Unit, University of Sussex, (1983)

34. Social Trends 1984, op. cit., p.190
35. Handy, op. cit.
36. Pahl, op. cit., p.2
37. Ibid. p.2
38. Warr, op. cit., p.305
39. Peter Warr, 'Economic Recession and Mental Health: A Review of Research', to appear in Tijdschrift von Sociale Gezondheidszorg, (1984)
40. Social Trends 1984, op. cit. In May 1983, a quarter of all claimants were receiving unemployment benefit and a supplementary allowance. Over half received supplementary allowance only (the lowest rate). Among the long term unemployed 86 per cent were getting supplementary allowance only
41. Robert Taylor, Observer Newspaper, (1 March 1981)
42. Warr, op, cit.,(1984)
43. Yankelovich, op. cit.
44. Ibid.
45. Adrian Sinfield, 'Unemployment in an Unequal Society', in Brian Showler and Adrian Sinfield (eds.), The Workless State, Martin Robertson, Oxford (1981), p.22
46. See Catherine Hakim, 'The Social Consequences of High Unemployment', Journal of Social Policy, 11.4, (1982), pp.433-67 for a review of available evidence on the consequences of unemployment for poverty; health and mortality; mental health; crime and delinquency; and the social fabric. Also Peter Warr, 'Work, Jobs and Unemployment', already cited and A. Charnley, M. Osborn and A. Withnall, Chapter 2 'The Impact of Unemployment' in 'Review of Existing Research in Adult and Continuing Education. Volume IX Adult Education and Unemployment', mimeograph, National Institute of Adult Education, (1982) for reviews of research relating specifically to the psychological effects of unemployment with comment on different subgroups of the unemployed population
47. Hakim, op.cit., p.444
48. H.M.S.O. op.cit.
49. R.Tyrrell and M.Shanks, 'Long Term Unemployment', Work and Society, London. (1982)
50. Op. cit., (1984)
51. Jimmy Barnes, 'Breaking the Malaise for our Jobless', BURN Newsletter No.4, (Spring 1984)
52. Olya Khaleelee and Eric Miller, West Yorkshire Talks about the Future of Work, Work and

Society, c/o National Westminster Bank, 210 Pentonville Road, London, N1 9JT
53. Jahoda, op. cit.
54. Warr, (1984), op. cit.
55. Warr, (1983), op. cit.
56. Peter Warr and Glennis Parry, 'Paid Employment and Women's Psychological Well-Being, Psychological Bulletin, 91, (1982), pp.498-516
57. Office of Population Censuses and Surveys: Labour Force Survey, 1981, H.M.S.O., London, (1982)
58. Hakim, op. cit., discusses the relationship between crime rates, delinquency and unemployment, concluding that unemployment in young people has definite associations with an increase in juvenile delinquency and crime
59. John Hill, 'The Psychological Impact of Unemployment', New Society, (19 January 1978), p.11
60. Ibid.
61. Peter Warr and Paul Jackson, 'Men without Jobs: Some correlates of Age and Length of Unemployment', Journal of Occupational Psychology, 57, (1984), pp.77-85
62. This section draws on that part of Hakim's (op. cit.) discussion about the social fabric
63. Hakim, op. cit., p.455
64. Ibid.
65. Ibid., p.456
66. Adrian Sinfield, 'Social Policy Amid High Unemployment', in C.Jones and J.Stevenson, (eds.), The Year Book of Social Policy in Britain. (1980-1981), RKP, London (1982)

Chapter Two

UNEMPLOYMENT AND THE ROLE OF EDUCATION

It is widely agreed that unemployment in the United Kingdom is too high. This was indeed the case in 1980 when the percentage of the labour force out of work, at 6.9%, was roughly half the 1985 figure. There have been many forces at work and many explanations of this situation. A demographic perspective would point to the increasing proportion of young people, meaning that entrants to the labour market outnumber those retiring. Another factor is that more women have become economically active in recent years for longer periods of their lives.

Others would point to changes in total output which have caused, or been caused by, the recession in world trade, over valuation of the pound or long overdue restructuring of basic industries with excess capacity. Productivity increases have had both short and long run effects. In the short term, new technology may directly replace some jobs whereas in the long term the increased wealth created by the same new technology may increase jobs in other sectors. Some effects are linked to rigid employment practices resulting in poor business performance and output lower than it otherwise could be.

There are those who lay the blame on the government's monetary and fiscal policies and the dominant need to control inflation. Restrictive policies have interacted with poor international competitiveness, there being mutual causation, to yield lower than necessary levels of economic output.

It is not our purpose here to review these explanations in detail nor to emphasise one at the expense of the other. The point is to look forward

Unemployment and the Role of Education

to see what they mean for the future. On the one hand, many economic forecasting groups see little change in the numbers unemployed through to the 1990s. The range of estimates is approximately 2.5 to 4.5 million people. Taking something of a middle road, the government sees growth in the rate of unemployment to be flattening out and then followed by a decline. For example, Lord Young, having identified a recent 'flat' trend in late 1985, suggested 'Continuing growth in the economy and falling inflation will help to keep new jobs coming.'[1] This statement followed a six month period in which the total unemployment among adults had risen by 94,500.[2]

A more optimistic perspective is based on the view that the government can manage the economy in such a way as to substantially reduce unemployment. If particular economic policies were the cause of high unemployment after 1979, then a reverse of these policies could reverse the effect. For example, having argued for a more Keynesian approach to economic management so that inflation and employment both become objects of policy, Henry Neuburger concludes, 'that the government can do something about reducing unemployment.'[3] But what of the position beyond the range of current forecasts? It is salutary to remember that, by 1990 the period of high unemployment will have exceeded ten years. This is longer than the period of high unemployment which spanned the first world war and which was the period during which many of the concepts and policies surrounding jobs and employment were developed in our society. Unemployment changed from a problem of social policy, what to do about the poor, to one of economic policy of how best to organise the labour market to increase its efficiency and decasualise work. Labour exchanges were set up in 1909 and unemployment insurance introduced two years later.

What is learned can be unlearned and replaced with new paradigms. It is not clear whether current rates of unemployment will eventually come down or remain a permanent feature of our society. However, holding one view or the other will lead to different definitions of the problem and therefore, different proposals for its solution.

Unemployment and the Role of Education

THE UNEMPLOYMENT 'PROBLEM'

For those who believe that high unemployment is temporary, it is a problem because economic imperatives and the work ethic decree that those who can do jobs should do so. Allowance needs to be made, of course, for certain 'exempted' groups such as housewives and chronically sick or disabled people. Those who do not have jobs are regarded as deviating from the norms of society. They should be contributing to the national wealth and their idleness, albeit enforced, means that they are a wasting and costly burden. From this perspective unemployment is viewed mainly in terms of the lack of paid jobs, those who are unemployed no longer being able to sell their skills, many of which are considered inappropriate to the present and future needs of industry. It is recognised that being unemployed is not a pleasant state and its financial consequences must be relieved by social benefit payments. However, whilst few believe that unemployment will disappear in the near future, it is still perceived as a temporary phenomenon. Given the 'right' policies, full employment will once again become the norm.

The alternative perspective is held by those who believe that unemployment is relatively permanent. From this point of view, unemployment is not, in itself a problem. It has become a problem because 'earning one's living', through doing paid work, is the only generally accepted way of ensuring a reasonably comfortable life and of getting the necessary work done for the good of everyone. There are few ways of achieving personal satisfaction other than by 'working for a living', unless, by private agreement, one or more persons share their income with others. Unemployed people do not only lack a job but, because of the constraints put upon them, they also lack any viable alternative way of ordering their lives and those of their families. They also suffer all the undesirable consequences of their situation described in the first chapter.

From this point of view, then, the problem becomes one of a different order. The first perspective is based on the assumption that full employment is the natural order of things, the problem, simplified, becomes that of how to create jobs and get people into them. In contrast, the second sees the problem mainly in terms of finding

Unemployment and the Role of Education

alternatives to the present very unsatisfactory state of being unemployed, alternatives which do not rely solely on notions of employment.

It is not suggested that these are the only ways of looking at the future of unemployment. The point is that they represent the extremes of a scale which encompasses the range of commonly held views. The solutions stemming from these assumptions are as opposed as the assumptions themselves and again they form a scale which encompasses a broad range. What is significant for this book is the way various assumptions might affect provision of appropriate education.

SUGGESTED 'SOLUTIONS'

Using a medical analogy, unemployment could be thought of as a disease. Now, the problems of a disease can be treated in two ways. One is to eliminate the factors which cause it. The second is to treat the symptoms. Clearly, if the causes of the illness are not eliminated, then treatment of the symptoms will need to be repeated from time to time or to go on continuously. So, with the problems of unemployment, solutions can be those which eliminate the causes or which alleviate or remove the symptoms. They can, of course, be a mixture of the two.

However, to go back to the medical analogy, there is often serious disagreement as to what causes particular diseases and, indeed, how to treat the symptoms once they do occur. Sometimes, a particular disablement is declared 'incurable', for instance, the loss of a limb. The challenge to society then is to accommodate these people in ways which do not discriminate against them, so that, they feel to be as 'normal' as, and enjoy all the same benefits as, any others who are not so affected. This requires, however, on the part of everyone, an acceptance that being disabled is not a problem. It is how disabled people are regarded and treated which is.

The solutions which are suggested to the problem of unemployment are very like the kinds of solutions which are posed to the problems of physically disabling conditions to which there is apparently no immediate cure. If there is the expectation that the causes can be eliminated in the

Unemployment and the Role of Education

not too distant future, then attempts to 'normalise' the condition will not be very strenuous. Effort will be aimed at containing the disease. Meanwhile, within the resources available, the patients are kept in as good a state as possible, with some help to alleviate the worst of the symptoms. They might be encouraged to keep as fit as possible in order to take the best advantage of the cure when it occurs.

If unemployment is considered to be 'incurable' in the sense that a well person is one who has a job for most of his/her life, then the analogy with a limbless person holds. The problem becomes one of attitudes and the way society reacts to those people who belong to a group about which the rest of society feels it can do nothing, now or in the future.

Analogies can be pushed too far, and this one has now served its purpose. What is clear from the different solutions offered for the problem of high unemployment is that they vary according to assumptions about its relative permanence as outlined in the two perspectives of the problem described above.

The assumption that high unemployment is temporary follows from a belief that unemployment is the result of worldwide recession, wrong economic policies and poor commercial competitiveness due to high wages, and the inflexibility of the workforce. Poor competitiveness may also be the result of lack of investment, poor management and marketing.

Whichever combination of factors is favoured, these problems are perceived as surmountable so that full employment should remain the ultimate goal. Therefore, it is vitally important that the workforce (employed and unemployed) should engage in training or retraining in order to have ready the skills required for present and future jobs and occupations. The response to the problem of the mismatch of skills to the projected demands of industry is to increase those forms of education which will make unemployed people more employable. Economic growth would be aided by having better quality staff at all levels and, later, would not be restricted by shortages of supply of trained recruits.

This set of solutions is being supported by government at present. For example, the 'Technical and Vocational Education Initiative' now introduces stictly vocational training to youngsters at a much

Unemployment and the Role of Education

earlier age than previously. Training for employment begins at 14. The 1984 Government White Paper 'Training for Jobs'[4] and the programmes of adult training supported by the Manpower Services Commission are intended to tackle the skills 'mismatch' problem with regard to adults. Proponents of these solutions argue that there has been a decrease in the demand for unskilled labour, a person's physical strength is no longer an asset. There is a need for a skilled and capable workforce to fill the jobs of the future, many requiring highly trained technicians.

Most people would agree that both education and training are required to equip youngsters and adults to undertake necessary work to provide goods and services for ourselves and to trade with others. What is debatable is whether training 'for stock', to be used at some unspecified future time, is a realistic strategy. Firstly, forecasting demand for labour at the level of detail required is extremely difficult. Secondly, such a strategy is likely to be unacceptable to most trainees. They are looking for enhanced prospects immediately on completion of the training and would not be satisfied with distant promises even if they believed they would come about.

Notwithstanding these problems, the assumption of future low unemployment means that the current position must be coped with and, as far as possible, skills and orientation to jobs not allowed to wither away. This is a major problem for the direction and management of training so that workers who leave the labour market of an old industry can re-enter a new industry and cope and contribute effectively.

The second perspective is that unemployment will not decrease to give full employment, as we know it, ever again. The implications of this are that unemployment can no longer be regarded as something to be avoided at all costs. The punishment, in terms of the consequences discussed in chapter one, meted out to people who cannot get paid work is no longer tenable. In such a future, there need to be redefinitions of the meaning of work, jobs and unemployment.

A possible solution lies in work sharing. This has several aspects ranging from shortening the working week to reducing the length of careers. Average weekly hours in major European countries fell by approximately 25% between 1960 and 1980.[5]

Unemployment and the Role of Education

There are many reasons for this, including reduced employment in industries where hours have traditionally been long, such as agriculture, and increased numbers of women doing part-time jobs. The view that employees might prefer shorter hours is supported by a European Commission survey which showed a majority in each member state, and 51% overall, in favour of shorter hours for the same pay rather than better pay for the same hours. The results of such surveys depend on their timing and respondents' perceptions of their future prospects. The possibilities of a rapid reduction in hours being acceptable remain unclear and the consequent economic effects uncertain. Employers' direct costs rise immediately yet there are subsequent compensatory changes in aggregate demand and taxation.

Reduced lengths of careers through both late entry and early retirement are possible. For example, Charles Handy advocates a 'job life' of some 50,000 hours.[6] This, allowing for 10% absenteeism each week, is the job of a professional officeworker who joins the workforce after university at 22 and leaves at 57. Compared to the 45 hours a week for 47 weeks a year for 47 years, worked by some people, making 100,000 hours of employment in all, this is just half. Halving the job life might mean spreading employment more thinly across the years. Alternatively youngsters may enter the labour market later and most workers could retire at 55 or even earlier. One of the problems of such proposals is that, in addition to the question of income redistribution which would be needed, there is the possibility of redistribution of the consequences of unemployment. Young and old may not suffer loss of status but they may lack access to opportunities for satisfying work.

Work sharing models are limited. Not only is it difficult to see whether they could be introduced quickly enough to make a difference but they also perpetuate the concepts of job and unemployment. At a simple level of analysis, life would be the same except with less work and more leisure. Others perceive second order changes. Peter Kelvin says,

> The one thing that the Protestant Ethic cannot survive is structural unemployment or systematic underemployment, because they effect... the structure of society itself.[7]

Unemployment and the Role of Education

For Kelvin, work could lose many of its central connotations. For Charles Handy,[8] people would work fewer hours and mix unpaid work and job work at various times. The role of contract worker, selling labour under self-employment arrangements, would replace full time employment. This would result in greater scope and freedom although, Handy does not add, there are echoes of the role of casual worker during Victorian or earlier times. Winters in the future may be as hard as in the past.

James Robertson,[9] describes five possible future scenarios. These are: (i) Business As Usual which views the future as much like the present and the past, with the same problems, conditions, changes, crises and so on. Nothing will change dramatically. (ii) Disaster, which assumes catastrophic breakdown, there being no realistic alternative to nuclear war with the famine, poverty, disease, crime and increasing unrest which will follow it. (iii) Authoritarian Control (AC), a view which has two variants - the left wing one and the right wing one. The right wing view is based on the assumption that the risk of disaster is very real. This implies the need for an increase in authoritarian systems of government, which will enforce law and order and distribute resources as is deemed best. The left wing variant of this view is one where reliance is put on authoritarian state control to create a better society. (iv) The Hyper-expansionist (HE) Future, a view which holds that through accelerating super-industrial drives, making more use of technological developments and science, we can break out of present problems. Use of nuclear power, space, computing and so on will enable constraints associated with geography and human frailty to be overcome. (v) The Sane, Humane, Ecological (SHE) Future, a more optimistic view, and one which does not rely on continuing acceleration and expansion, but relies on achieving a balance within ourselves, between individuals and between people and nature. It gives top priority to living supportively. This will involve decentralisation rather than more centralisation.

In Tony Watts'[10] four scenarios, the first three - continuing high unemployment, increased leisure and increasing employment - are presented as unacceptable. Firstly, high unemployment maintains groups of haves and have-nots with all the associate problems of control. Secondly, significantly more

Unemployment and the Role of Education

leisure begs the question of whether leisure can fulfil the same latent functions as employment. Thirdly, an employment orientated future requires new employment and job sharing. The jobs that are created may not be satisfying and there would remain problems of enforcement. Watts' fourth scenario includes a mixture of formal and informal economies as well as leisure. Changes in the ways in which people's status is defined are required and these echo some of the features of Robertson's 'sane, humane, ecological' future.

None of these authors is making a forecast although they are not averse to expressing preferences. They are painting pictures of the choices facing society and what might come about if certain policies are followed. It is not our purpose to add more scenarios or to forecast or choose between them. Rather we seek to establish that a number are possible and desirable.

If high unemployment is temporary, and the 1980s come to be regarded as a passing phase, then well and good. One major element of social stress would be removed. If, on the other hand, high unemployment is permanent, then the quicker that new attitudes, definitions and relationships emerge the better. Education must play a role in creating and understanding these new relationships.

EDUCATIONAL IMPLICATIONS

If unemployment is perceived as temporary, a result of a mismatch between demand for and supply of labour and skills, then solutions will involve training and retraining of individuals to meet changing labour demands. These responses will be within the present framework of social and economic structures with conventional employment still viewed as the norm.

Some macro-economic policies will be expected from governments who may be held responsible for some of the economic decline. However, activity will mainly focus on individual members of the labour market. They will be expected to change as required by the varying demands of industry and commerce. They may also be expected to 'create their own job' through self-employment initiatives.

Meanwhile, whilst unemployed they must have a basic survival kit of welfare benefits with advice

Unemployment and the Role of Education

on how best to make a little money go a long way. In addition it is now becoming recognised that unemployed people may usefully take part in a whole range of voluntary and other types of unpaid activities. These may help to combat the adverse social and psychological effects of being unemployed, while at the same time keeping them active, alert and in good health.

Within this perspective, the educational system also has a role in training unemployed people to cope with their present situation. They could gain by becoming more self-reliant, doing things for themselves which they might otherwise have to pay for. This needs to be balanced against the possibility that self-sufficiency, as Jonathan Gershuny[11] points out, can have problems. In the self-service economy more services, both domestic and leisure, are provided by machinery within the home. This can reduce social contact through work and increase isolation.

The education system can also provide classes to enable unemployed people to develop hobbies and leisure interests, the basic stuff of adult education, and thus keep them active and employable whilst they wait for the job market to improve. It can provide opportunities for inceasing computer literacy and awareness of new technologies. Not least it can improve the literacy and numeracy skills of those unemployed adults whose general education finished at an early age and which left them ill-prepared for a world of increasing bureaucracy and high technology, a world of abstractions, of numbers, codes and graphs.

In contrast, if unemployment is considered to be relatively permanent or to occupy significant periods of people's lives, then the concept of training becomes too narrow, as indeed do those traditional educational structures which rely on the ideas of 'teachers' and 'taught'.

If unemployment is interpreted as a family, community and societal issue, one involving employment and work in general, rather than something only those defined as unemployed experience, then the concept of education will need to be very broad, including ideas of self-help, learning exchange, community and political action and so on. Responses to this perspective will need to emphasise useful activity which is not necessarily paid work, and which is not seen as

Unemployment and the Role of Education

merely treating the psychological depression of the unemployed. They will need to tackle the desire for individuals to have a personally satisfying life as well as one which enables them to feel part of their community and society. There will need to be a blurring of the boundaries between home, work and leisure and the implications of this for income and the distribution of wealth. Opening up a debate about work and the future would be part of this.

Educational provision to help the problem of unemployment depends upon the particular view the providers hold and the interpretations that unemployed people themselves put upon their situation. As far as unemployed people are concerned much will depend on the age, sex, occupational status, previous work experience and how prevalent unemployment is in a particular locality, as well as how long a person has been unemployed. So, some unemployed people will regard their state as temporary and others regard it as permanent. Some will feel they themselves are to blame whilst others will blame the economic system or "society".

Attitudes towards unemployed people are confused and sometimes deeply contradictory. There are accusations of twisting the benefit system, people being better off unemployed than working. There is blame for government policies with accounts of whole communities becoming unemployed when a large works shuts down. There is, not surprisingly a division of opinion about whether 'the unemployed' are any different from anyone else in their educational needs. For example, the range of non-vocational 'interest' classes provided throughout adult education and by institutions such as the WEA are as relevant to unemployed people as to anyone else. There is, however, a large number of people without permanent employment in a social system based on work and in which status is fixed by occupation. Given the evidence in chapter one, our argument is that there is a definite need for educational provision tailored to suit the special needs of this particular group.

The suggested causes and consequences of unemployment will obviously influence the content and form of such provision. The foregoing discussion however, leads to the conclusion that any form of educational provision should be judged against the following general aims. Any educational provision for unemployed adults should:

(i) take into account the different assumptions about the nature of unemployment and therefore the possible solutions,

(ii) reflect the needs which are common to the majority of unemployed people as evidenced by the effects that unemployment has on them, and

(iii) appreciate the individuality of unemployed people who react to their situation in ways specific to them, their families and communities.

These aims for educational provision for unemployed adults do not define in detail the content and form that provision will take. They do, however, imply that the responses of 'educators' will need to be wide ranging, flexible, accessible and above all built on unemployed people's individual needs in the context of family and community as well as the wider debate about the future of work and society.

Challenging existing structures, in particular those related to jobs, should be regarded as important as helping people cope with current problems of rent, literacy, welfare or getting a job.

NOTES

1. Lord Young, Secretary of State for Employment, quoted in The Guardian, (31 January 1986)
2. Central Statistical Office, Monthly Digest of Statistics, (February 1986)
3. Henry Neuburger, 'Why is Unemployment So High?', National Westminster Bank Quarterly Review, (May 1985), p.13
4. Government White Paper, Training for Jobs, HMSO, (January 1984)
5. OECD, Economic Outlook, (September 1983)
6. Charles Handy, 'Work, Life and Money - A New Arrangement', in Gabriel Fragniere (ed.) The Future of Work: Challenge and Opportunity, Van Gorcum - Assen/Maastricht, The Netherlands, (1984)
7. Peter Kelvin, 'Social Psychology 2001', in Robin Gilmour and Steve Duck, (eds) The Development of Social Psychology, Academic Press, (1980), pp. 296-297

Unemployment and the Role of Education

8. Charles Handy, <u>Taking Stock. Being Fifty in the Eighties</u>, BBC, London, (1983)
9. James Robertson, <u>The Sane Alternative</u>, Robertson, Ironbidge, England, (1983)
10. Tony Watts, <u>Education, Unemployment and the Future of Work</u>, Open University Press, Milton Keynes, (1983)
11. Jonathan Gershuny, <u>After Industrial Society: The Emerging Self-service Economy</u>, Macmillan 1978

Chapter Three

CURRENT EDUCATIONAL RESPONSES TO ADULT UNEMPLOYMENT

This chapter classifies and reviews the responses made by agencies and institutions to the educational and other needs of unemployed adults. A variety of sources have been drawn upon. There is a range of reports, some of which are concerned with the needs of unemployed adults,[1,2,3,4] while others include provision for this group within the arrangements made for adults generally.[5,6] In addition, the authors have, in a series of interviews with unemployed people and those working with them, gathered first hand information about some more specific attempts to provide relevant learning opportunities for unemployed adults. Finally, in April 1984, one of the authors, on behalf of the Community Education Section of the Open University surveyed all local education authorities, university extra-mural and polytechnic adult education departments, as well as the Workers Educational Association in an attempt to ascertain the nature and extent of educational programmes provided specially for unemployed adults.

TYPES OF PROVISION

There are both a great number and variety of agencies and institutions which provide, or enable others to provide, education for adults - that is, 'educational training undertaken after leaving full-time initial education (i.e. schooling followed immediately by entry into further or higher education)'.[7] In order to cope with this variety, reports have typically created some form of

Current Educational Responses to Adult Unemployment

classification to be used as the basis for comparison and discussion.

Typically, the classification is based on the nature of the agencies providing the facilities. Percy et al. in their report on post-initial education in the North West of England,[8] give a taxonomy of providers and agencies as follows:

* Public authorities including local education authorities, responsible bodies, libraries,
* Leisure sponsors and social services, universities and direct grant colleges, mass media
* Voluntary organisations at national, regional and local levels, both those created for an educational purpose and those with other purposes as well
* Vocational training agencies such as the Manpower Services Commission, industrial training boards, Confederation of British Industry and Trades Union Congress education departments, trade unions, professional associations, armed forces
* Community development agencies, that is community associations, neighbourhood councils, community arts and education ventures
* Private agencies such as correspondence colleges, private local schools (e.g. driving, music, language, office skills etc.).

This taxonomy groups providers according to expected degrees of similarity of ethos within the organisations. For example, public authorities are likely to see continuing education as an extension of provision made in schools and colleges. Vocational training agencies will seek to serve a client set of current and potential employers and provide courses on the basis of manpower planning. Community development agencies will view education as a possible element in a process of change. Private agencies will have profit as their prevailing ethos.

There are other classifications of providers. The 1982 ACACE survey 'Adults: Their Educational Experience and Needs'[9] lists:

* Further education college/technical college
* Local education authority
* Evening institute/adult education centre

41

Current Educational Responses to Adult Unemployment

* University extra-mural dept/polytechnic/Open University
* Community centre
* Women's institute/townswomen's guild/women's clubs
* Sports centres
* Workers Educational Associations
* Government/DES
* Trade union

This is a less comprehensive classification with more specific categories. It illustrates the difficulty that the desire to make specific comments and comparisons between types of provider must be balanced against the problems, in practice, of an example falling into more than one category. For example, work carried out in technical colleges may also occur in polytechnics. Yet again, in many areas the Workers Educational Association makes joint provision with university extra-mural departments.

Each of the above taxonomies refers to providers of education for all adults. However, provision is often made exclusively for, or at least aimed towards, unemployed adults. For instance, in the report of Charnley et al into education for this group, the following types of providers were identified:[10]

* Manpower Services Commission
* Local Education Authorities and University extra-mural departments
* Trade unions and the Trade Union Congress
* Employers
* Voluntary agencies
* The broadcasters

In the Northern Ireland survey,[11] the following were given as making some kind of provision for unemployed adults in Northern Ireland:

* Colleges of further education
* Higher education institutions
* Workers Educational Associations
* Library service
* Department of Economic Development (through Government training centres, Attachment training schemes, schemes for specific groups e.g. redundant managers or well qualified 'A' level people).

Current Educational Responses to Adult Unemployment

Neither list refers explicitly to those special centres which have sprung up in recent years in response to high levels of unemployment. These provide advice, help, various facilities or simply somewhere for unemployed people to go. Charnley et al[12] include these under the 'Voluntary Agencies' heading.

Such is the growing number and wide geographical spread of these initiatives, however, that they have come to be recognised as being both important and different. A useful classification ought to include them, not as a separate group, but according to form and purpose. With a variety of names such as 'drop in centres', 'resource centres' to 'centres against unemployment', these initiatives are rarely direct providers of formal education and training but can act as facilitators for other organisations.

So far we have discussed the possibility of a typology of providers based on the nature of the agency or institution making the provision. This is, however, a limited, one-dimensional approach which may fail to capture other aspects of variety. An additional form of analysis could, therefore, be made of users of the service provided both in terms of the type of people they are and the role which they are expected to fulfil in the educational process. For example, educational institutions of the conventional type have the basic philosophy that all who can benefit from a course have a right to join one, and that, on joining, they take up the role of a student. On the other hand, training agencies seek people who have aptitudes which can be developed by training to fulfil labour market needs. Consequently, participants become trainees.

Yet another dimension, related to the target group and participant's roles, is the learning mode. The context of the learning, from classroom to workshop, and the style from teaching and training to facilitators are important differences in the nature of provision.

A further aspect concerns the way in which the provision is managed. The goals of the provider and the organisational form will display considerable variety. Publicly owned educational institutions will be concerned with making greatest use of limited resources and ought to have appropriate bureaucratic management. On the other hand, voluntary agencies may devote much effort to securing resources and be less concerned with control.

Finally, recognition can be made of the range of outside interest groups who, in addition to the direct providers and participants, have a stake in the success of the initiative. In the case of training agencies, these stakeholders are employers. Community projects may partly serve the interests of tenants' associations or political parties and will certainly serve the local community. Some voluntary initiatives may seek only to satisfy the needs of the members themselves and have few, if any, other stakeholders.

This discussion has shown that, while classification by provider or sponsor seems to be prevalent, there are other scales along which similarities and differences between initiatives can be identified. These dimensions are users, learning mode, management and stakeholders. They are, however, not independent for Percy et al showed how the first three additional items can be shown to correspond to the different classes of provider.[13] Figure 3.1 is based on Percy's typology with the addition of the dimension of stakeholders who may have important interests in the success of initiatives without having to pay for them.

In the following description and discussion of the numerous examples of initiatives, the typology of Figure 3.1 is used. Attention is drawn to the relationship between the various dimensions included in Figure 3.1, particularly the way in which management provides a context for the user to learn about the content of whatever education is being provided.

Content, Form and Context
As a preface to the discussion of educational provision for unemployed adults, mention needs to be made of certain constraints on the ability of unemployed people to participate. These, in turn, affect the nature of provision for them.

Under the DHSS rules, anyone claiming unemployment or supplementary benefits cannot undertake any educational course which lasts for longer than 21 hours per week. Study for longer than this is judged to be a negation of the 'availability for work' condition for receiving welfare benefits of the kind described. Thus an unemployed person who wishes to study full-time, must forego any benefit

Figure 3.1: Typology of Post-initial Education Agencies (based on Percy et al.)

	Type I Educational Service Agency	Type II Participant Member Agency	Type III Training Programme Contracting Agency	Type IV Community Project Developing Agency	Type V Private Sector Agency
SPONSORSHIP					
Finance	Allocations from central and departmental budgets	Local and regional mixed funding (self help plus subsidy)	Programme budgeting systems	Project budgeting (with supervision)	Profit-margin budgetting
Legitimations	Public service ideologies stressing learning, process values	Philanthropic ideologies: stressing collective and altruistic values	Managerial ideologies: stressing design and product values	Participation ideologies: stressing community and self-awareness values	Market ideologies: stressing 'value for money' values
MANAGEMENT					
Focus	Deploying given resources within imposed limits	Mobilising members or volunteers to secure provision	Meeting cost and effectiveness	Developing a strategy for social animation	Identifying and filling market gaps
Form	Bureaucratic management plus professional elements	Elective representative management plus advisory elements	Corporate management	Idiosyncratic management	Commercial management
USER					
Market	Universal entitlement but specified priorities	Bringing together of those of similar interests	Specified training target groups in specified numbers	Positive orientation to the culturally and educationally deprived	Supplying demand where profit can be maximised
Status	Learner	Member	Client	Participant	Customer
LEARNING MODE					
Context	Class	Club	Course	Workshop	Group/home learner
Style	Teaching	Skill exchange	Training	Facilitation	Instruction
STAKEHOLDERS	Public authorities, community as a whole	Members	Employers, MSC, Trades Unions, DHSS	Community groups, political parties	Owners

Current Educational Responses to Adult Unemployment

received and find an alternative form of income. Full-time courses provided specially for unemployed people are usually those funded by the MSC. In these cases the participants normally receive an allowance and travelling expenses. It is sometimes possible for unemployed people to be grant-aided by LEAs to attend a full-time course, but these grants are discretionary and are not at all widespread. Of course, any person may apply for a statutory grant to study full-time in higher education.

The 21 hour rule affects the type of study possible. Most of it must clearly be of a part-time nature and, whether it is part of an institution's general provision or not, any person undertaking such study must be prepared to give it up if the offer of a suitable job is received. With this in mind, we turn to the first member of Percy's typology.

Educational Service Agencies
The description in Figure 3.1 indicates that much local education authority and public sector provision would be of this type. This includes classes run by further education colleges, adult education centres and polytechnics. Most of the university extra-mural provision can also be described in this way - teaching by professionals in the context of a "class", even though the venue might be outside the formal learning institutions.

Three modes of provision can be distinguished. Firstly, the courses and classes which are generally available to any adult. Joan McDonald reports comments made by some staff in adult education.

> ...when asked what was being done for the unemployed, (they) pointed out that there were unemployed students over the whole range of their provision, but that they did not, and did not wish to distinguish them from other students or to create what were often referred to as "unemployed ghettos".[14]

Provision available to unemployed people in this way includes what are traditionally known as non-vocational as well as vocational courses. Unemployed people themselves do not always make distinctions such as these and may use non-vocational classes for job related purposes as

Current Educational Responses to Adult Unemployment

well as attend a craft or technologically orientated course for interest only.

Some of the general provision will attract more unemployed people than others. For instance, literacy and basic education courses have always had a significant proportion of students who were unemployed. The variety of courses coming within the general category of "Second Chance" education, though catering for a variey of students do include many who are unable to get paid work. In their flexibility of attendance patterns and curriculum, the inclusion of personal guidance and counselling, and continuity of provision which allows entry at different levels of ability, these courses are particularly attractive to those unemployed people who lack many basic and social skills.

The second mode of provision is what is known as "in-fill". This allows unemployed people to take "partial" courses, attending some classes in a course but not others. Some colleges and institutions have a designated member of staff responsible for negotiating in-fill arrangements with other staff and unemployed people presenting themselves for education. It is quite often the case that registered unemployed people get partial or total remission of fees. Clearly, in-fill can only work where there are vacant places and staff who are sympathetic to the particular situation that unemployed people find themselves in. This type of provision varies from institution to institution and place to place in the country. Joan McDonald notes:

> It was also noticeable that departments such as engineering, where courses and students had declined in numbers because the local industries, which in the past their courses had served, had collapsed, readily welcomed the unemployed. By contrast, departments which could still be expected to see their students employed at the end of the course, such as catering, rarely had room for them.[15]

The third mode of provision is that which is specially designed for adults who are unemployed and which usually responds to that particular characteristic. The provision may be special in that the content is thought to be particularly relevant to those who are unemployed, or the pattern of provision is such that it fits in with the style of

Current Educational Responses to Adult Unemployment

living of someone who does not have to "go to work". Both the content and form may be tailored to particular target groups within the main category of people who are unemployed. For instance, particular age groups, women or those whose first language is not English.

An unpublished survey of provision specially designed to meet the educational needs of unemployed adults, carried out by one of the authors on behalf of the Community Education Section of the Open University,[16] found that the content of that provision could be categorised as follows:

* Welfare rights/unemployment related issues
* Life and study skills /self-help
* Issue based classes/discussions (e.g. social policy, local issues, expressed needs)
* Subject based classes/discussions (e.g. history, economics, psychology)
* Interest classes/courses (creative writing, visual arts, media, music, drama, physical exercise, health, recreational pursuits, arts and crafts (non-vocational))
* Foreign languages
* Computing
* Employment skills (e.g. craft/technician/ office training, management skills, back to work for women)
* Small business
* Job getting (e.g. job search, application, interview)
* Educational/training advice/counselling.

All LEA institutions, university extra-mural or continuing education departments, polytechnic departments of continuing education and Workers Educational Associations were contacted.

Out of the 175 responses made by LEAs throughout the UK, 130 institutions said that they made some kind of special provision for people who were unemployed. Preliminary results show that the most frequently mentioned types of provision are:

* Life and study skills/self-help skills
* Employment skills
* Job getting skills
* Interest classes/courses.

Current Educational Responses to Adult Unemployment

Of these, life and study skills, which includes basic education, were mentioned twice as often as any of the others. However, there is some doubt in the case of some of the responses whether this type of course is provided specially for unemployed people - it is likely, however, that most of the students are unemployed. If the three employment related categories (employment skills; small business; job getting) are taken together, they account for a substantial amount of the provison. Computing courses and educational advice and counselling account for moderate amounts of provision. There is very little specific provision for welfare rights courses, those dealing with unemployment or other social and local issues, and subject based classes. None of the LEA institutions mentioned foreign language teaching.

The results of this survey can be compared to the report (covering all sectors of education) prepared by Joan McDonald,[17] which mentions under the heading 'Subject matter':

* Courses to help people become self-employed (not restricted to unemployed people)
* Basic education
* Job seekers courses
* Know your rights courses (LEA and WEA provision, often done by volunteers on a one-to-one drop-in basis in unemployment centres)
* Health, diet and budgeting (often focused on women)
* DIY (courses, one-day sessions, drop-in basis)
* Creative writing (often as part of basic, post-basic and 'second chance' education)
* Music and dancing (attractive to young people, sometimes orientated to ethnic minorities)
* Sports (attract a mainly male clientele).

McDonald's report does not indicate how widespread each type of provision is and as she rightly points out the situation is not static - initiatives are made, some continue, others are discontinued for lack of resources or support. This needs to be borne in mind when considering the ACACE report on Education for Unemployed Adults. When this report was published in 1982, the chapter headed 'What

Current Educational Responses to Adult Unemployment

adult educators are doing now: some examples', included in its introduction the statement, 'Most of the initiatives examined in this evidence were experimental and many have as yet hardly got under way'.[18] The report describes the following types of provision:

* Mainstream courses
* Coping with changed circumstances (self-help groups, applying for jobs, early retirement, keep fit, grow your own food, drop-in advice)
* Maintaining and developing skills
* Use of practical facilities
* Creative activities
* Understanding unemployment (mainly University and WEA provision)
* Basic education
* English as a second language
* Small businesses
* Co-operatives
* Access/bridging courses

It is unclear just how far this provision is made specially for adults who are unemployed although much of it is clearly relevant to them.

The 1983 report of the Northern Ireland Council for Continuing Education says of the specific provision made by Colleges of Further Education in Northern Ireland, 'Only a few further education colleges reported that they had initiated courses specifically for the adult unemployed (as distinct from providing courses on behalf of another agency).[19] In fact, it goes on to say that a majority of colleges do provide courses at the request of bodies such as the Department of Economic Development and Industrial Training Boards. However, these courses relate mainly to the secretarial and office field. They appear to be full-time, of 12-18 weeks duration and participants receive a training allowance. The comment is made that '...the number of these courses had reduced drastically over the past few years and the Working Party views with concern this reduction in training/education opportunities for the unemployed'.[20]

Regardless of whether special provision is made for unemployed people or not, there are variable practices regarding educational advice and counselling of a wider nature. For instance, at the time of writing, anyone enrolling on the course

Current Educational Responses to Adult Unemployment

specially provided for unemployed adults at one of the Community Colleges in Leicestershire is individually interviewed and given ongoing support and counselling throughout their time as a student there. Students are encouraged, with the advice of tutors, to choose their own subjects and a certain amount of experimentation is expected before they settle down to their particular choices. Students attending this course appear to welcome the opportunity to study in the company of others who are unemployed as well as themselves. Some have formed a self-help group which meets once a week.

Another college in Lancashire aims to transfer students, after an initial 12 weeks preparation, into mainstream courses on an in-fill basis. A lecturer has been given special responsibility for recruiting under the 21 hour rule and for giving students advice and being their main contact whilst they study there. At other places, although the normal advice service is available, there is no special consideration given to anyone who happens to be unemployed. Some staff at some institutions consider that making special provision for unemployed people only serves to increase the stigma that unemployment brings.

Changing perceptions of the nature and needs of users have encouraged agencies to develop provision which is more user centred. In this way the Type I providers begin to resemble Type III as the status of users and the learning mode move towards the member and club variety. For instance the Victoria Project at Gravesend in Kent links the educational facilities available at the main adult education centre with those which have been acquired as a drop in centre for unemployed people. Members attend classes in the main centre with some, who have particular skills, acting as voluntary tutors in the Project centre itself.

There is sometimes the opportunity for students to plan their own programme of learning to a limited degree. In one of the Inner London Authorities, a course, planned for women only, allows individuals to assemble their own timetable within a supportive group framework. This does not, however, mean a free for all situation. There are some formal requirements of belonging to the group such as study skills for everone every Friday morning and the expectation that each member would go to at least four classes a week. On the other hand, schemes may

Current Educational Responses to Adult Unemployment

be formally designed like the job preparation course in one of the adult education institutions in Birmingham. Being in the centre of a large Asian community, the formal curriculum at this unit reflects Asian interests but has many white students also. A unit such as this sometimes gets students who are in danger of losing their benefit because their lack of language skills mitigates against their satisfying the condition of 'availability for work'. Their attendance can be used as evidence when claiming welfare benefits with the DHSS.

Two examples of the use of schools for unemployed people are the 'Parents-school partnership' and the 'Return and Learn' programmes in Liverpool. The parents-school partnership brings parents and other adults into primary schools to interest them in education. A room is made available for the use of people in the neighbourhood. There are coffee mornings and social activities, also basic education and recreational classes. Some people go on to take basic secondary school level qualifications. At the time of writing, seventeen primary schools were involved with plans to include ten more. Several comprehensive schools are also opening up similar home-link opportunities.

The Return and Learn project encourages young adults without jobs to return to school and pursue some educational activity suited to their needs. The only formal conditions are a six month interval since leaving school and the participant's lack of employment. The average age of people participating in this scheme has risen throughout its life and there is no formal upper age limit. In 1984 the number of teachers working in 14 school based centres was expected to rise to 70, with the students numbering 600. The maximum number of hours of study for any participant is 21 hours so that the availability for work criterion is not breached.

Provision for unemployed adults can take place outside educational institution premises, in libraries, church halls, leisure, youth or community centres, voluntary centres and unemployment centres.

Two examples from higher education are those devised by Wolverhampton Polytechnic and the University of Leeds. In 1984, the Centre for Unemployment Studies at Wolverhampton Polytechnic's project involved two groups of unemployed people recruited through a house to house survey. They were meeting in their own localities for two hours a week

Current Educational Responses to Adult Unemployment

for a period of ten weeks. The programme included discussion about unemployment and its effects, training in job getting skills, benefits and rights, activities, leisure and health. It also looked at financial budgeting at a national as well as a household level and finally explored a number of possible alternatives to conventional employment. At the time of writing this programme had just come to an end. It had been run on a 'one-off' basis, financed by the local authority, as an experiment which was to be evaluated in order to make proposals for possible future provision.

The project undertaken by the Department of Adult and Continuing Education at the University of Leeds is more extensive than the Wolverhampton one and of a different kind.[21] Funding of £13,500 for 1982/3 from a DES grant with an additional £16,000 from the University enabled a programme of 116 courses, with an average of 10-12 students, to be mounted in Leeds and Bradford during that academic year. The programme has continued to be funded, but at a reduced level (£18,500 for the 1983/84 academic year). The courses (generally 2 hours per week for 8 weeks) are in the 'liberal adult education' category, including welfare rights and courses aimed specifically at women. The organisers of the programme collaborated with other educational institutions, churches, organisations such as unemployment centres set up specially to help those who are unemployed, community groups and trade unions.

The intention of both Wolverhampton Polytechnic and Leeds University is that, in part, they should act as catalysts for further activity. It is hoped that the Wolverhampton groups will continue, even though the formal programme has finished. The Leeds project has already been partly successful in this aim, some of the classes having been taken over by adult education and one by the Citizens Advice Bureau.

The University of Leeds project, however, is not typical of the generality of University provision. The Universities Council for Adult and Continuing Education Working Party on Education for the Unemployed,[22] in its survey of provision made by extra-mural departments concludes that 'only seven departments (Bristol, Durham, Hull, Leeds, Manchester, Surrey and Ulster), can be said to be heavily involved in making course provision

53

specifically for unemployed people in the sense that staff are committed to that work over a number of years, as distinct from departments which may offer one or two courses as marginal offerings.

Of these, Bristol and Manchester are mainly concerned with education or training for re-employment funded by the Manpower Services Commission. Durham and Hull, as well as Leeds are linked with a variety of local and other agencies. As a result of collaboration with the Director of Education on South Tyneside, the LEA and the WEA, Durham University has received funding from the Inner City Partnership programme to pay for the salary of a development officer and a number of part-time tutors.

The initiatives by the Industrial Studies Unit in Hull University Department of Adult Education are described by Daniel Vulliamy in the journal 'The Industrial Tutor'.[23] Early activities by the Unit were carried out in collaboration with local trade unions, the Trades Council, Hull City Council and Humberside County Council. A voluntary body which was established at that time 'Hull Unemployed Education Project' submits proposals for courses to the Industrial Studies Unit and to the WEA. This body has also been successful in raising money to pay for unemployed students' travelling expenses.

According to the UCACE report,[24] Leeds and Surrey are the only departments to receive special DES funding which is sufficient to support full-time staff on course provision specially for unemployed people. Where no external funding is received, departments must meet the cost of any special programmes out of their normal budgets. Many do allow unemployed people to take courses free of charge or at a reduced fee. These costs also have to be borne by the university concerned, a cause of great concern.

Of the small provision generally that is made by universities, the author's survey indicates that the proportion of university provision related to welfare rights and unemployment issues is higher than in further and adult education institutions, but is still overall quite small. Life and study skills are also represented but not to the same proportionate extent as for LEA institutions. A few courses only are related to employment skills (3 on management skills and 3 on wider opportunities for

Current Educational Responses to Adult Unemployment

women) with, as expected, more provision of 'interest' type classes.

The Northern Ireland report says of higher education institutions in Northern Ireland, 'It would appear that these institutions are assessing much more closely the needs of the adult unemployed'.[25] The Derry Unemployed Education Project arose out of a pilot scheme, organised towards the end of 1981 by the Institute of Continuing Education, Magee University College, co-operating with the Northern Committee of the Irish Congress of Trade Unions. The situation in 1984 was that this group was flourishing being directly aided by the New University of Ulster and the Northern Ireland District of the Workers Educational Assocation.

Established in November 1981, there had been a total of 1,357 enrolments to April 1984. The type of courses provided by the project fall into three main categories: adult basic education, social and life skills, and useful skills/recreational pursuits. Evidently, the group felt initially that courses specifically related to the unemployed should be provided. When participants' confidence had been built up, they could then be filtered into existing courses. Some money (£800 in 1984) was available to pay students fees to attend courses at the New University of Ulster and the Technical College. Ulster Polytechnic has provision for unemployed people to sit in on elements of different courses, and also makes special provision of courses for starting up a business, acquiring study skills and money management.

Polytechnics throughout the UK are on the whole well disposed towards mature students. They often run part-time courses of one kind or another and are therefore used to having adults as students. This also means that they have experience in devising schemes of study which do not require full-time attendance. There is often a generous attitude towards course entry requirements, many having close links with local further education colleges who 'feed' them students deemed capable of following a Polytechnic course, but who do not have the formal entry requirements.

At least seven polytechnics operate MSC funded courses designed specially to meet the needs of unemployed adults. Other polytechnics, for instance Oxford, Manchester and South Bank, have developed

55

Current Educational Responses to Adult Unemployment

courses, programmes and activities which are not funded by the MSC. Both Oxford and Manchester have arrangements with local colleges to allow them to feed in students to their specially flexible arrangements. At least one of the Polytechnics has an unemployed graduates club.

The Polytechnic of the South Bank has created an extra faculty, called the 'Extra Faculty Unit' which has a number of units concerned with those who are unemployed. One called 'SHAPE' is a course organised around the 21 hour rule. This appears to attract people with a managerial or professional background. Students have a choice of both structured courses and less structured workshop and project activities. Members of SHAPE have access to all the facilities of the poytechnic, including sports. They have in addition, their own common room with a typewriter, a telephone and tea making facilities. There is regular counselling, students being helped with self-assessment and career planning.

These examples have been included to show that there is a number, perhaps small, of initiatives which, although made by one of the traditional providers of education, are not of the type of teaching normally found there. As previously mentioned, this provision begins to resemble Percy's Type II.

Participant Member Agencies

Type II agencies include many of the voluntary and more informal types of educational provision. The Workers Educational Association is an example of this type. A national voluntary association, it is funded by the DES and to a smaller extent by LEAs. These grants cover some of the costs, the remainder being met by fee income and other voluntary sources. The local branches which do not receive money from public funds, and which involve members who are representative of the students, provide the voluntary effort required to promote their local programmes. Several branches make up a district which does have a small full-time staff. There are 21 WEA districts.

The WEA has been, and is active in making special provision for unemployed adults, in the majority of cases free of charge to the participants. Tutors have been made available to work with unemployed people, often in unemployment

Current Educational Responses to Adult Unemployment

and community centres, the WEA rarely having premises of its own. The implictions of this are a commitment, on the part of the organisers to raise funds from voluntary donors. As with the provision made by Type I agencies, unemployed adults attend WEA classes which form part of the general provision as well as those which are designed to meet their special needs.

From October to December 1983, HM inspectors carried out a survey of Workers Educational Association provision for unemployed adults[26]. The survey covered nine WEA districts involving 29 courses, some of which included more than one class during a full day. Thus, 37 class units were visited. These are categorised in the report as follows:

* Welfare rights
* Return to learning
* Counselling in groups
* Courses directly related to unemployment and re-employment
* Art, drama, writing, photography, current affairs

No indication of the relative extent of these different kinds of provision was reported except for the comment that the number of courses which 'could be said to make a direct approach to the task of improving the present situation of unemployed adults or seeking novel ways out of that condition'[27] is small.

In contrast, the author's survey, which included the WEA, found, as might be expected of an institution devoted mainly to providing liberal education, that the most frequently mentioned category was 'interest'. These courses include creative writing, visual arts, media, music, drama, physical exercise, health, recreational pursuits, non-vocational crafts. The second largest category of provision was 'welfare rights/unemployment issues', the split within this category being approximately equal between welfare rights and unemployment issues. Life and study skills courses, together with issue based discussion classes make up the bulk of the remaining provision.

According to the HMI report[28], welfare rights courses are generally open to all although much of the time is spent in giving advice to individuals who have particular problems. Much of this provision takes place in unemployment centres and can involve volunteers who are themselves unemployed.

The 'Return to learning' courses often involve students meeting for ten weeks or more. These courses are generally "student-centred" incorporating elements of choice and catering for different levels of educational experience. There is often a core curriculum with other parts being offered on a "menu" system or negotiated between tutor and students. These courses are generally conducted with a minimum of formality so that there is ease of access for anyone wanting to take part. "Return to learn" courses include elements of basic education (literacy and numeracy), communicating, study skills, creative writing and work of a project type nature. For instance the Milton Keynes course includes project work based on issues relating to the city itself.

Students may go from these kinds of courses onto more formal study at a higher level. However, as Joan McDonald notes of these courses generally, not just those provided by the WEA,

> ...students who have gone on to higher education from courses of this kind have usually been accepted by faculties of humanities and social studies. It is less usual to find "Second chance" provision in science and technology.[29]

It is interesting that the Inspectors' report[30] categorises 'counselling in groups' as one type of WEA provision. This is described as, '...a series of meetings under the guidance of a tutor, at which the interests of the members form the agenda, or curriculum'.[31]

Out of these unprogrammed activities might arise specific activities such as co-operatives, workshops, drama groups and local studies projects. Comparison with LEA or higher education institutions is difficult to make. The impression gained from personal surveys and the McDonald report[32] is that students interests can be identified. Thus:

> Many project workers stressed that the unemployed needed what they called a "sorting out" period, which gave them time to assess themselves and their situation, and to

Current Educational Responses to Adult Unemployment

> experiment. This could be done through group discussion, with support and counselling, sometimes combined with educational "sampling" where the group was based on a college or centre.[33]

Survey evidence suggests, however, that the WEA does not provide much which is solely of an advice or counselling type.

Comments have already been made about the WEA provision which addresses issues related to improving the present position of unemployed adults. Although the DES report[34] states that there are only a small number of these courses, they still significantly outnumber those provided by LEAs and higher education institutions.

The WEA in Edinburgh has an interesting course for unemployed adults lasting eight to ten weeks. Since 1981 there have been at least seven of these courses held in comfortable premises in the centre of Edinburgh. The course takes place on Fridays from 9-30 a.m. to 3-30 p.m., students bringing their own lunch to eat together in the canteen. Colin Kirkwood and Sally Griffith's book[35] describes how unemployed people's needs were identified and how the subsequent course evolved.

> From an initial pattern which emphasised student choice, yet by the same token excluded options not chosen we gradually evolved a pattern of four key curricular components:
> Human relations
> Writers' and readers' workshop
> Society and politics today
> Maths or arithmetic.[36]

They say that these are the areas which the majority of students have shown most interest in. The course is regarded as a package of inter-related parts and students are encouraged to attend all of it. However, because of timetabling pressures, the maths and arithmetic had to be moved to another day and is now part of a new open programme offered on that day. This programme allows students to opt for single classes which include a history project, an exercise, health and relaxation class and a writers' workshop concentrating on spelling, punctuation and grammar.

Alongside the Friday basic programme and the open programme, there has evolved a follow up programme which includes discussion of unemployment and trade unions as well as a welfare rights class. The topic of running a small business, included at the very beginning as part of the pilot course has been dropped entirely, there being little student interest in it. The content of provision within the Edinburgh course mirrors that of WEA provision generally. It is an example of a well thought out course based on the perceived needs of unemployed adults having few, if any, educational qualifications or specific job skills.

It is this key consideration that distinguishes Type II from Type I. The WEA, for example, has a philanthropic rather than public service ethos which means that users' needs are paramount. Type I agencies, on the other hand, have to balance the demands made by a range of stakeholders into a more general 'public service' commitment.

Comment has already been made that WEA classes for unemployed adults often take place in unemployment centres. As providers or facilitators of education these centres are reminiscent of Type II agencies but more nearly approximate to Type IV agencies, that is 'Community project developing' agencies and it is to these that we now turn.

Community Project Developing Agencies

Funded as initiatives encouraging involvement of unemployed people in a variety of social and learning opportunities, helping each other morally and practically, these agencies exist in a variety of contexts. Accommodation may be provided by statutory or voluntary organisations, sometimes consisting of a single room but in some cases being self contained suites. The centres may be available to unemployed people for a few hours each week or be open continuously. The groups of unemployed who use the centres may participate fully in the decision making processes regarding the aims and organisation of them. Some centres have paid supervisors or coordinators whilst in others the members themselves carry out the planning and organising often on a rota basis. Clearly, if a group of unemployed people use a centre which is sponsored by an educational institution, there is a greater chance of some educational provision for this group being made.

Almost all unemployment centres provide a welfare rights advice service, usually on a personal basis. Many of the organisers also see their role as

Current Educational Responses to Adult Unemployment

one of giving advice on other matters of personal and practical concern to those using the centres. Depending on sources of funding, there are different emphases on, for instance, provision of workshop facilities to maintain and improve skill or campaigning for a better deal for unemployed people in their struggle to get jobs. Groups who receive funding from the MSC are not allowed to carry out any activities which could be construed as 'political'. Where a group is funded through local or county councils, activities may be constrained in different ways, depending on the department of the council which is responsible for the control of funds. An education department may wish to prevent conpetition with existing facilities or an employment department may look for results in terms of the establishment of new businesses, whereas social services may be concerned with the alleviation of stress.

Much of the 'success' of these centres in recruiting people who are unemployed to use them in providing interesting opportunities for learning depends on the skill and experience of those who carry out the organising functions. As Joan McDonald says,

> The character of the latter[37] differed very considerably in composition, organisation and intentions. Some had begun with a dynamism which could not be sustained. ...Some were inexperienced in organisation and in handling funds....However, some independent groups were functioning very effectively, meshing in with the existing local community organisations ...Some negotiated with LEAs and the WEA for vocational and educational courses. Some successfully applied for funding to provide educational and technical equipment in their own centres.[38]

Thus, whilst workshop facilities might be available in centres, the extent of organised professional tuition varies greatly. A centre in Whitehaven has the majority of the week timetabled to provide tuition in many different activities. Another centre in Sheffield, runs its woodwork and upholstery workshops on a drop-in, self-service basis. The Adult Learning Project in Edinburgh, reflecting the theories of Paulo Frere, encourages local people to define their own learning needs as a group within a community. A specific project of ALP is a skills exchange which enables participants to do needed tasks for each other but, more interestingly, form learning pairs or groups where members share skills and knowledge.

Both Type II and Type IV provision share the feature of being orientated to the needs of the member or participant. In contrast to the content and form of these types, there is the important Type III Training Programme Contracting Agency in which the user is cast in the role of client receiving a defined service which will give improved prospects in the competitive labour market.

Training Programme Contracting Agencies
The budgeting, organisation, focus and ideology of these agencies show significant differences from other forms of provision. Programme content is likely to be clearly prescribed, attendance patterns insisted upon and cost-effectiveness used as a major measure of success, particularly in terms of employment placements.

The agencies firstly define the type of training which they wish to see provided. They might, then, carry out the training themselves. However, it is often the case that they buy it from any recognised institution or organisation which has the required staff and resources to supply it. Examples of these agencies are Employers' Associations and employers themselves, Her Majesty's Forces, Industrial Training Boards, the Trades Union Council, and the Manpower Services Commission.

In Northern Ireland, the Department of Economic Development and the Industrial Training Boards sponsor specific courses for the adult unemployed. These are provided by the further education colleges. Indeed the Northern Ireland Council for Continuing Education's report says 'Only a few further education colleges reported that they had initiated courses specially for the adult unemployed (as distinct from providing courses on behalf of another agency).' But, 'a majority of colleges provide specific courses for the adult unemployed in co-operation with, and at the request of, other statutory bodies, e.g. the Department of Economic Development and Industrial Training Boards'.[39] These

Current Educational Responses to Adult Unemployment

courses tend to relate mainly to the secretarial and office work field, recruitment being carried out by the sponsoring body. The report indicates that the Department of Economic Development was offering (in 1982/3) training/retraining programmes for approximately 1,100 unemployed people, that is about 2% of the basic skilled/unskilled unemployed in Northern Ireland.

In England, Wales and Scotland, the Manpower Services Commission is funding, on a large scale (the Government's white paper 'Training for Jobs' mentions £250 million per annum) job training and retraining programmes. The MSC makes very little direct provision, but buys training from whoever it considers can supply it economically and effectively. Through its 'Open Tech' programme, courses are provided for technicians, managers and supervisors. These allow a mixture of face-to-face teaching and home study with flexible study arrangements. However, these courses are not restricted to the unemployed, and it is probable that they are of more value to those people already in jobs than those who are unemployed.

A large part of MSC funded provision is that which comes under the heading 'Work Preparation Courses'. A review by the Adult Training Branch of the MSC[40] gives the aims of work preparation as enhancing the general employability of unemployed people lacking basic skills.

> It provides assessment, improves general work-related skills, trains in job-getting skills, and rebuilds motivation. Where married women have decided to return to employment, it seeks to make re-entry more efficient.[41]

The scale of provision is large in comparison with Type II and Type IV agencies. In 1983/4 12,236 people were involved in work preparation courses at a total cost of £17.9 million. In addition 572 women (total cost £0.38 million) were participating in 'Work Opportunities for Women' courses.

The 1984-1988 MSC Corporate Plan[42] outlines two new programmes which, whilst retaining the work opportunities courses, build on and replace current adult training programmes. These are (i) a programme of job-related training and (ii) a programme specifically designed to help unemployed people. The latter aims to improve unemployed people's

Current Educational Responses to Adult Unemployment

foundation skills and retain their employability, that is to maintain their motivation and abilities needed to seek and do a job, or undertake further education or training. It is intended to spend some £55 million on this programme and £190 million on the programme of job-related training.

Some of these courses are (or will be) available on a full-time basis, participants being paid a training allowance. Others might be full or part-time with only fees and expenses paid. In particular, any training which is provided as part of work within the MSC's Community Programme is likely to be of a voluntary nature with fees/expenses only paid.

Towards the end of 1984, the Department of Education and Science supported by the MSC and the Welsh Office, initiated a three year programme of educational provision for unemployed adults. Entitled 'Replan', its aims are 'to promote the development of educational opportunities for the adult unemployed'[43]. The National Institute for Adult and Continuing Education has been given responsibility for employing and managing a team of field officers to advise and help those agencies who wish to make some kind of educational provision for unemployed adults. Money (£2.5 million over the three years 1985-1987) is available to fund specific projects. At the time of writing, 78 applications for funds had been made - the majority focusing on outreach work, educational counselling and non-vocational courses and crafts[44]. It should be mentioned, however, that this situation could change as time goes on.

The Manpower Services Commission has declared its intention[45] to co-operate with the 'Replan' initiative, particularly in the areas of information and guidance to unemployed people, training provision as part of work within the Community Programme and curricula development. Thus, although the MSC will buy training from wherever it sees fit, not only from official educational institutions, it still appears willing to collaborate with adult education in this context.

The final category of provision, Type V Private Sector Agencies, includes those which supply training to MSC specifications and derive much of their income from this source. There are also private schools and colleges.

Current Educational Responses to Adult Unemployment

Private Sector Agencies
These providers seek to make profit from the provision of education and training. Users take on the role of customers within a market. Unless funding is supplied by sources such as the MSC, clients will have to bear the fees. In consequence, many agencies are orientated towards the needs of unemployed managers and professionals. Emphasis is often on job getting skills such as preparing CVs, interview behaviour and job search generally. Sometimes firms will pay for training of this kind for employees who are about to be made redundant.

CONCLUSION

This chapter shows that the responses of the educational system to adult unemployment are many and varied. Of the taxonomies which have been proposed, one was selected and developed as a means of classifying and describing these responses. Important dimensions along which comparison could be made are providers, users, learning mode, management and stakeholders. These dimensions are not independent of each other, however, and we have shown how links are made. For example, provision made by training programme contracting agencies is likely to involve narrowly selected classes of participants in clearly prescribed learning situations. Management of these agencies is likely to have a placement generation orientation with its efforts aimed at satisfying employers as major stakeholders.

Categories are not hard and fast. Initiatives have secondary outcomes in addition to their primary functions. For example, activities directed towards passing public examinations often involve participation in groups with their consequent social benefits which are incidental to the main purpose.

Much of the thrust in provision is in both conventional education for learner clients and conventional training for trainee clients. In each case the satisfaction of public, stakeholder needs comes first and individual needs second. How far individual needs are recognised and responded to depends on the constraints imposed by the primacy of public needs.

Recognition of the special needs of unemployed adults only takes place at the margin. Where

Current Educational Responses to Adult Unemployment

something can be done at low cost, and no penalty to other groups of participants, then there are efforts made. As we have shown, some of these can be very useful and imaginative. Yet the private needs of the unemployed remain hardly recognised and hence hardly responded to. Rules, especially the 21 hour rule, mean that many openings are not available. Long courses require long term commitment. An unemployed person will have to think twice before participating in long courses. This is because it would involve an admission that the state of unemployment is likely to last for some time.

Some organisations have gone a long way to recognise these issues and respond accordingly. We have described arrangements where level of participation and content of units are open to negotiation. These initiatives can still appear to be modifications of conventional systems. They seek gradually to bridge the gap between potential learners and conventional provision by moulding the learner into standardised forms. After an initial induction period it becomes business as usual from the provider's point of view.

It may be that something more radical is required. In Chapter six we will show how experimental projects, not necessarily set up within educational contexts, can have important learning consequences. Yet we will note that these do not fall easily within Percy's taxonomy as the expected relationships between various elements no longer hold. We may have to search outside that framework in order to find opportunities which are most likely to satisfy the needs of the adult unemployed.

NOTES

1. See A. Charnley, M. Osborn and A. Withnall, <u>Review of Existing Research in Adult and Continuing Education, Volume IX, Adult Education and Unemployment</u>, National Institute of Adult Education, Leicester (1982).

2. <u>Education for Unemployed Adults</u>, Advisory Council for Adult and Continuing Education, Leicester, (1982).

3. <u>The Educational Needs of Unemployed Adults</u>, Northern Ireland Council for Continuing Education, Bangor, Co. Down, Northern Ireland, (1983).

Current Educational Responses to Adult Unemployment

4. Joan McDonald, <u>Education for Unemployed Adults: Problems and Good Practice</u>, Department of Education and Science, (October 1984).
5. <u>Adults: Their Educational Experience and Needs</u>, Advisory Council for Adult and Continuing Education, Leicester, (1982).
6. Keith Percy, Stephen Butters, John Powell and Irene Willett, <u>Post Initial Education in the North West of England: A Survey of Provision</u>, Advisory Council for Adult and Continuing Education, Leicester, (1983).
7. <u>Adults: Their Educational Experience and Needs</u>, op. cit., p.1.
8. Op. cit. see pp.5-6.
9. Op. cit. see p.33.
10. Op. cit. see section 4.1, pp.46-61.
11. Op. cit. see pp.14-17.
12. Op. cit.
13. Op. cit. p.221
14. Op. cit. p.17
15. Ibid. pp.18-19
16. This was a questionnaire asking about special provision for unemployed adults, sent to relevant education officers in all LEAs in the UK, as well as to University extra-mural departments, Polytechnic departments of continuing education, and the district officers of the WEA. The responses have been analysed only in so far as the type of provision is concerned. These have not yet been published.
17. Op. cit. pp.23-25
18. Op. cit. p.12
19. Op. cit. p.14
20. Ibid. p.15
21. See the report 'Beyond Tokenism', obtainable from the Department of Adult and Continuing Education, University of Leeds
22. University Council for Adult and Continuing Education, <u>Working Party on Education for the Unemployed</u>, UCACE, (September 1984), p.2
23. Daniel Vulliamy, 'Educational Provision for the Unemployed', <u>The Industrial Tutor</u>, Vol.3, No.5, (1981), pp.73-76
24. Op. cit.
25. Op. cit. p.15
26. Department of Education and Science, <u>Report by HM Inspectors on Workers Educational Association Provision for Unemployed Adults</u>, DES, (1984)
27. Ibid. p.10

28. Ibid.
29. Op. cit. p.22
30. Op. cit.
31. Ibid. p.8
32. Op. cit.
33. McDonald, op. cit. p.23
34. Op. cit.
35. Colin Kirkwood and Sally Griffiths, (eds), *Adult Education and the Unemployed*, Workers Educational Association, (1984)
36. Ibid. p.160
37. By 'the latter' is meant those groups which exist on an independent basis
38. McDonald, op. cit. p.28
39. Op. cit. p.14
40. *Review of Work Preparation Courses (including Wider Opportunities for Women Courses)*, MSC's Adult Training Branch internal paper - concerns courses run from 1982 to 1984, Paper given to author in November 1983
41. Op. cit. p.15
42. MSC Corporate Plan for 1984-1988
43. See Department of Education and Science leaflet, *The New Further Education and Training Initiatives - a guide for employers*
44. Communication with a research officer of the National Institute for Adult and Continuing Education, preliminary unpublished data
45. These intentions were stated during one of the 'Replan' regional conferences held in November 1984

Chapter Four

THE INADEQUACY OF THE CURRENT SITUATION

Chapter three described and classified the range of educational programmes, courses and classes made available to unemployed adults. Some are provided especially for unemployed people, whereas in others the students have a variety of personal circumstances. Chapter two argued for the requirement for provision that was tailored specifically to the needs of those who are unemployed. The purpose of this chapter is to critically review that type of provision and also to discuss non-specific education where relevant.

Chapter two concluded by specifying three general aims that education for unemployed adults should try to achieve. These were that any educational provision for unemployed adults should:

>(i) take into account the different perspectives on what constitutes the problem of unemployment and therefore the possible solutions.
>(ii) reflect the needs which are common to the majority of unemployed people as evidenced by the effects that unemployment has on them.
>(iii) appreciate the individuality of unemployed people who react to their situation in ways specific to them, their families and communities.

In addition to these aims, it was stated that the responses of educators should be wide ranging, flexible, accessible and reflect both an individual's needs and the wider debate about the future of work and society.

The Inadequacy of the Current Situation

In examining the balance of current provision this chapter starts by comparing it with the first two of the above general aims. Discussion of the third aim comes later when the question of access to opportunities is considered.

It has been established that unemployment is not merely the lack of a paid job, but the absence of work in its wider sense. The future may bring a return to 'full' employment or it may be one where fundamental shifts in the notions of jobs, careers and related status structures take place. The former suggests provision of employment related education to prepare people for the opportunities to come whereas the latter implies education for survival, coping and, hopefully, alternative advancement and change.

It is too much to expect that all possibilities could be addressed in all situations. We would expect to find programmes and courses which aim directly at helping participants to become more employable and also provide training to meet the needs of sectors in the economy where there is demand for labour.

We would also expect there to be educational opportunities where participants can enlarge their horizons as well as explore and resolve personal needs and their roles in the community. Such opportunities could include a search for alternatives, a striving for social change, an understanding of the causes and consequences of unemployment as well as evaluating and disseminating learning concerned with survival, coping and adaptation.

EMPLOYMENT RELATED PROVISION

Implicit in the concept of education for employment is the assumption that unemployment, viewed as the lack of paid jobs, is brought about by the decline in demand for particular types of labour. At the same time, the absence of supply of other types of labour restricts the expansion of demand. As mentioned in Chapter two, the implications of this are that there exist amongst unemployed people a large number who no longer have the skills required by industry and commerce at the present time. The logical outcome is, then, that any educational responses to the needs of unemployed people are

The Inadequacy of the Current Situation

likely to be linked to the concept of training and retraining, that is, the Type III provision of chapter three. Not only that, but it is also supposed that those who are unemployed will be able to get jobs more easily if they improve their job search and job getting skills.

An earlier paper written by one of the authors,[1] concluded that most of the provision concerned with education for employment - training in job getting skills, computing and training courses in other job skills- took place within mainstream further and higher eduction. The responses to the Open University survey of special provision for unemployed adults, discussed in chapter three,[2] show that this still appears to be the case, with job skills and job getting skills being provided for equally, certainly as far as local authority educational institutions are concerned. Clearly, where equipped laboratory and workshop facilities are required, job skills courses are mostly found within the further and higher education sectors, where they have, in the past, had the budgets to provide them. The Manpower Services Commission has sponsored many courses providing training in these sectors -the Government White Paper "Training for Jobs"[3] mentions a figure of 80,000[4] unemployed people involved each year in MSC training programmes. It is possible to deduce from the comments in Joan McDonald's report[5], that in fact, the majority of employment oriented education and training courses - those directly related to acquiring job related skills - are those sponsored by the MSC. For instance, in her section on programmes specially designed for the unemployed she makes no mention of any with subject matter related to acquiring employment skills, e.g. craft, technician, office training, management skills and so on. This omission, coupled with the comment, "....this enquiry was directed to education and not to training"[6], when referring to the role of the MSC supports this conclusion.

We have pointed out that the WEA, does not make any but the smallest employment related provision.[7] However, within many of the unemployment centres there can be found various workshops which can be used in a number of different ways from casual through to formal timetabled arrangements. The latter approach is, however, rare and workshops are

The Inadequacy of the Current Situation

generally used for do-it-yourself activities as individual needs arise.

As well as the specially provided courses, there are the infill arrangements within the mainstream provision found throughout the further, adult and higher education sectors. However, Joan McDonald's report clearly shows that infill arrangements are far from ideal and the 21 hour rule precludes attendance on full-time courses. As shown in chapter three, infill arrangements are more readily available on courses where regular demand is low, such as engineering, than on courses where career opportunities are still available, such as catering. Therefore, from the point of view of providing improved career prospects for participants, as well as increasing the supply of suitably qualified personnel, infill arrangements are likely to be only marginally successful.

It is increasingly the case, with the cutting of budgets in all sectors of education, that it is to the MSC that attention must turn to find the sponsorship for any extension of employment related education and training. The Government has set out its adult training strategy, which the MSC will manage, in the white paper "Training for Jobs".[9] This reports that the MSC proposes the restructuring of its training provision for adults into two main programmes:

> (a) An industry-focused programme for both employed and unemployed people, which would give them job-related training directed to known employment needs in industry and commerce and to helping the growth of businesses.

> (b) Giving further help for unemployed people who need training at a more basic level, particularly to restore their chance of getting a job after long periods of unemployment.

The Commission proposed to implement these proposals experimentally in 1984-85 with the main restructuring occurring in 1985-86. The White Paper says, 'We endorse this strategy as entirely in line with the market-oriented approach to training that is now required.'[10] It is envisaged that the total number trained each year will be over 250,000 of whom 125,000 will be unemployed, and the government is allocating some £250 million to this end.

The Inadequacy of the Current Situation

It is also expected that adults employed (often on a part-time basis) on the Community Programme one year's employment scheme will be offered the chance, on an expenses paid only basis, to participate in some type of linked training or work preparation course.

Is This Appropriate?
These developments in the supply of training to satisfy the needs of the labour market raise some important questions of appropriateness. Is there enough provision? Should the MSC be the agency for taking this kind of initiative? Does it meet the needs of unemployed people?

The adequacy of provision is questionable. Much of the effort is directed towards people already in employment. Projections are for 125,000 unemployed participants, somewhat fewer than 4% of the total registered unemployed, let alone the total number of all unemployed people. The programme may well meet the needs of industry and commerce, but it will take a long time to provide training opportunities for all those who are unemployed. As a provider of employment related education, the MSC is taking an increasingly dominant position. The White Paper proposal was for it to guide or direct 25% of vocational courses within the non-advanced sector of further eduction. The National Association of Teachers in Further and Higher Education has severely criticised the role of the MSC as proposed in the White Paper. The centralisation of decision making about training needs is considered totally inappropriate, ignoring knowledge held by Further Education colleges themselves about local employment conditions, their links with local employers and so on. Criticisms[11] of MSC control of training include comments that it is an instrument of cheap labour, it divides academic from vocational education, the monitoring of its schemes is virtually non-existent and it poses a serious threat to democratic control. In the words of Conall Boyle,

> Autocratic decisions will replace the tenuous democracy of boards of governors and academic boards. Broadly based education courses will be scrapped in favour of narrow "modular" two-week courses designed to meet the perceived short-term market needs of local employers. Price competition will determine course

The Inadequacy of the Current Situation

> placement......Faced with a 50-60% job placement criterion, many of the traditional 'speculative' FE courses (CGLI and BTEC) face extinction. Funds will be switched from colleges to employers, from areas of high unemployment to areas of (relatively) low unemployment.[12]

The emphasis in the White Paper on the needs of employers, the phrase, '...the decisions as to who is trained, when and in what skills are best taken by employers....',[13] and the insistence on investment in training needing to be financially attractive to employers, '....including the acceptance by trainees of levels of income which reflect the value to them of the training given...',[14] serve to justify these fears.

There is no way the request from the Government to the Commission, 'to extend its range of operation so as to discharge its function of a national training agency',[15] can be ignored. However, as already said, much of the proposed effort will be towards those people who are already in jobs. What relevance has education for employment got for those unemployed people living in areas of high unemployment whose chances of getting a job at the end of it are still fairly low? Therefore, a very important part of the question of appropriateness is whether this type of provision now, or in the future, meets the needs of those who are unemployed from their point of view as those affected most in the present situation.

It is clear that employment continues to be a major life goal, in spite of the poor job prospects in many areas of the country. For example, on the basis of a survey of what 152 unemployed people in Londonderry, Northern Ireland want, John and Sue Munday say, 'The work ethic still rules'.[16] Over 75% of their sample indicated a first preference for activities to improve their chances of employment. 'On the face of it, respondents saw education more as a means to secure employment and cope with being unemployed rather than just keeping occupied',[17] a finding supported by the survey of educational needs of unemployed adults carried out in 1982 by the Northern Ireland Council for Continuing Education.

Unfortunately, there appears to have been no large scale survey of the educational needs of unemployed adults in Great Britain. McDonald's report on provision does not address the issue of

The Inadequacy of the Current Situation

whether existing educational provision for unemployed adults is adequately meeting their needs, at least in any direct way. What she does say, is:

> There is little doubt that the majority of the unemployed would define good practice in education as education which leads to a job. (but) ...Students should be made aware that while education can improve employability, it cannot provide a job.[18]

On this issue, it is salutory to look at a survey by Daniel[19], of approximately 4000 unemployed people selected on a random basis. The interim report of the survey includes the reactions of the people questioned to training opportunities and other MSC services. Daniel says, 'In fact, formal training and retraining have traditionally played little part in provision for the unemployed in Britain and it is unlikely that they would ever be relevant to more than a minority.'[20] To be fair, however, he does then offer the somewhat contradictory statement that, 'Our present research shows that there is a substantial amount of both latent and manifest demand for training opportunities.'[21]

Evidence for this lies in the 49% of Daniel's respondents who said they had thought of undertaking training. However, only 31% stated that they had seriously considered it. This leaves 51% of those interviewed who had not thought of training at all. In fact only 14% of the whole sample had made any application to participate in a training programme. Those who had already some formal qualifications, educational or occupational, were more likely to apply for further training.

The respondents in Daniel's survey had only been unemployed a short time and therefore might be considered still to be in the 'optimistic' stage of unemployment referred to in chapter one. They had not resigned themselves to the patterns and status of unemployment. Even so, training did not appeal to a substantial number of them. They thought it to be more appropriate at later stages in unemployment if they failed to find work. However, it is precisely at these later stages, when depression and resignation have set in, that someone who is unemployed finds it even more difficult to take such an initiative.

The Inadequacy of the Current Situation

The White Paper 'Training for Jobs' in its second paragraph says,

> But training is not an end in itself. It is a means to doing a good job of work for an employer or on one's own account. Training must therefore be firmly work-oriented and lead to jobs.[22]

Do unemployed people perceive training as leading to jobs, and does it actually lead to jobs?

Daniel's survey revealed three main reasons why just over half the unemployed people in his sample had not considered training. These were:

(i) age, being too old (especially among those over 44 years old)
(ii) lack of knowledge or awareness of training opportunities (particularly among women and the young)
(iii) already being in possession of skills, liked the work they did and didn't want to train for another type.

The following comment is illuminating,

> Associated with those who reported that they already had skills were a disturbingly high proportion who said they had already done a training course. They like many of the young felt they had really had enough of training or education for a while and wanted 'a real job'.[23]

Common criticism of publicly available training opportunities were that there was no guarantee of a job after training and the fear that it would not improve prospects of employment.

The reaction of those people who had only given the idea of training a passing thought was that, although they thought they were lacking in skills, they expressed doubt that taking a course would really improve their employment prospects. Clearly, the common sense of most people, in areas of high unemployment at least, tells them that undergoing training is unlikely to alter the number of jobs available, they would merely be being trained 'for stock'.

The Inadequacy of the Current Situation

There are apparent contradictions here. People with qualifications seem to be more likely to take further training yet many saw job prospects as not being improved by training. It could be that qualified people value education for its own sake while those with less experience take a more instrumental view. Daniel's work brings out the perceptions of unemployed people. Another approach is to examine the performance of courses in achieving their employment aims.

The 'Work Preparation' courses are sponsored by the MSC to enhance the general employability of unemployed people who lack basic skills. In 1983/4 12,236 people were involved in these types of courses, the cost being some £17.9 million. In addition, the Wider Opportunities for Women (WOW) courses of a similar kind attracted 572 women.[24]

A review of the Work Preparation and WOW courses run in 1982/3[25] indicated that the majority of people taking part in the work experience courses are male, young, and have been unemployed for more than a year. Women on WOW courses tend to be older than women on the other courses - less than a fifth under 30 years of age - with the majority having been unemployed for over 3 years.

Of these participants, obviously a minority of unemployed people generally, only 19% had got jobs within 3 months of doing the course and 15% had gone into further training. This fairly low rate of employment, compared for instance to a 42% placement rate for the more specific job skills "Training Opportunities" courses, is to be expected. Such results, while suggesting that some participants benefited from the courses, will clearly tend to reinforce the perceptions of those who believe that training will not lead to jobs.

It would be easy to be persuaded that the MSC's new 'Adult Training Strategy' might prepare unemployed people for the requirements of industry now and in the future. This may be so, but is clearly of little use if the jobs for which they are being prepared do not materialise. Responses such as these certainly take into account the first of the major perspectives outlined in chapter two, that is that there will eventually be a return to full employment. It is clear, however, that they touch only a minority of unemployed people who might improve their competitiveness in the labour market at the expense of others who are or will become

The Inadequacy of the Current Situation

unemployed in their place. These responses are not, therefore, a reflection of the needs common to the majority of unemployed people.

It has become fashionable to state that a solution for many unemployed adults lies in self-employment - the spate of business start up courses might give hope in this direction. Starting and running a business successfully is, however, a complex affair. A whole range of skills is required, not just those relevant to one or two tasks. Some people might prosper in this way, but they will need more than just one course on how to be your own boss. They will need continued support to engage in a process of constant learning for many months after the business is formed. Clearly, the classroom mode of teaching is inappropriate to meeting these kind of needs.

The foregoing criticisms quite obviously cannot deny the necessity for education and training for employment. The vast amount of further education aimed at this purpose in the past has never been questioned, at least on its overall purpose. What is different now is the assumption implicit in the way this kind of provision is now being espoused. Lord Young said, 'I believe our failure to gear education and training sufficiently towards the requirements of employment is a major obstacle in the path of enterprise'. (Lord Young, at the time, Minister without Portfolio and former chairman of the Manpower Services Commission)[26] The assumption is that the major change required is by the individuals who are unemployed, as if it were all their own fault. It is assumed that 'they can somehow be extracted from their previous experience and culture and, whilst being provided with a basic survival kit of literature and advice on welfare rights, be transformed to fit a different labour demand model'.[27] However, there is little sign of any increasing demand for the labour of those who are unemployed, particularly if they have been unemployed for some time. John Hughes writing in the Child Poverty Action Group Journal says, with respect to young people:

> 'The transformation from school to work' is a phrase which now signifies not only a technocratic, logistical problem of efficiently introducing young people to existing job opportunities but also a profound social,

The Inadequacy of the Current Situation

> political and ideological dilemma in fostering a commitment to the principle of wage labour amongst large numbers of young people who are simultaneously denied access to it.[28]

This sentiment is equally applicable to unemployed adults. A report of the CEDEFOP conference on 'Continuing education and training for the long-term unemployed' says:

> The idea that training produced jobs was not subscribed to.....The earlier optimism that training would lead to jobs had dissipated. There was a realisation that people needed something more than job training if they were going to survive long-term unemployment.[29]

In the past, a major element of the motivation to continue in education beyond the school leaving age was the expectation of getting a better job. Few people would offer themselves for courses not related to their immediate interests and needs. The idea of being trained for a job or career which may not materialise is not tolerable to most people, let alone those who are already debilitated by the experience of unemployment described in chapter one. The overwhelming problem of employment related education is that unemployed people's needs are defined solely in terms of the supposed needs of industry and commerce. Little attention is given to the need for those without jobs to be convinced that there is any real understanding of the serious psychological and social problems that their situation imposes upon them. This is not to say, however, that there are not some very sincere attempts, in different parts of the educational system to give people who are unemployed skills to help them to cope better with their situation - it is time now to consider these.

EDUCATION FOR SURVIVAL AND COPING

Mention has already been made of the 'Adult Training Strategy' launched by the MSC in November, 1984, the second part of which focused on the needs of adults who are unemployed. An MSC press notice reporting a speech by the MSC chairman, states that this 'programme is specifically designed to help

The Inadequacy of the Current Situation

unemployed people improve their basic skills, retain employability and cope with the changing content of jobs and patterns of work.'[30]

From this perspective, many unemployed people are assumed to need education to improve their literacy, numeracy, communications and social skills. McDonald's report[31] comments that basic education has come to occupy a central postion in work with unemployed people, much in cooperation with MSC funded courses. These courses not only offer help with basic, social and life skills, but also offer participants opportunities to sample different jobs - a process known as 'job rehearsal'. She says, 'It is a tacit assumption that basic education will increase employability'.[32] Thus, learning about surviving and coping in this sense is learning how to 'remain employable'.

Examination of the responses from the Open University survey,[33] shows that the single most frequently mentioned category of provision for unemployed adults within LEA institutions is 'Life and study skills/self-help' which includes basic and 'Second Chance' education. It is probable that no great distinction is made between unemployed students and others in this category, but the majority are in fact people who have no jobs. This type of provision stands out in that the concepts and methodology used have' provided a pattern and an example for the development of work with the unemployed'.[34]

Individual responses to the Open University questionnaire show that there are some imaginative and useful courses which come under this heading. Both Further and Adult Education institutions have made great efforts to identify the needs of students who are unemployed and to tailor provision to these needs. Many incorporate an initial period of counselling and self-assessment giving participants time to assess themselves and their situation and to experiment with different learning modes. There is an acceptance that, as the participants in a course or class change, then the content of the learning must change also.

There is an appreciation that those who are unemployed, in particular the long-term unemployed have special needs related to the psychological and social effects of being unemployed. For instance, a report from the University of Durham[35] on work with

The Inadequacy of the Current Situation

unemployed people on South Tyneside, lists the following:

* Loss of confidence in their ability to find new opportunities in work, training and the educational field.
* Loss of motivation and an increased sense of hopelessness, especially for the over-40s.
* Loss of skills from their previous work and alternative occupations.
* Increasing loss of touch with formal and informal work contacts and job finding
* A significant need for retraining which is impeded by the lack of necessary educational qualifications and knowledge.
* The need to be able to think realistically of alternative occupations, in related or totally new fields.

Even so, underlying this statement of needs is still the 'increasing employability' belief. This is fine, so long as there is a chance of participants getting jobs on completion of their learning. However, care needs to be taken so that participants view this type of learning as useful in life generally, not just for the purpose of getting a job. Otherwise, those who leave these courses and then do not get jobs, are going to feel they have failed once again. Stressing employability may be a good way of 'selling' the courses, but could have unintended consequences for some people later on.

Regardless of this, it must be said that the long operational experience of many of the 'Second Chance' (Return to Learn, New Horizons etc.) courses developed as they have been, under the auspices of adult education in local education institutions as well as institutions such as the WEA and the extra-mural departments of universities and polytechnics, has influenced their "philosophies" in the direction of enabling people to fulfill their potential in every aspect of life, not just those which relate to paid work. The emphasis on encouraging participants to negotiate their own curricula and excercise control over their own learning processes is to be commended and is highly relevant to those who find themselves in a situation compounded by poverty, lack of education and discrimination in the labour market. Helping unemployed people to become emotionally stronger and

The Inadequacy of the Current Situation

more practically able to cope with unemployment is desirable, notwithstanding the accusations of 'merely providing palliatives' made by some critics. However, this type of educational provision will do little to alleviate the poverty and debt which many find themselves in.

Financial Survival

Surviving unemployment usually means managing with little money. Thus, getting full entitlements within the unemployment and supplementary benefit systems is of great importance. The amount of benefit reckoned to be unclaimed is very large. On the face of it, however, it appears that provision of 'Welfare rights' or 'Know your rights' courses is not very great. It is the WEA which seems to be most active in this sphere. The report by HM Inspectors[36] on the WEA provision for unemployed adults comments that this kind of work has become a part of most unemployment centres. It is certainly common to find professional tutors or voluntary workers engaged in individual counselling and advising in this area.

This advisory activity often takes the form of merely giving information although in some cases advisers act on behalf of their 'clients', mediating between them and the benefit offices or assisting them to prepare appeals. Either way, it may simply transfer dependence on one set of 'experts' (i.e. DHSS and Unemployment Benefit Office staff) to dependence on another (i.e. advisers). In spite of the best intentions, it is very easy to regard people who are debilitated both mentally and physically, as described in chapter one, as needing 'looking after'. The tendency then is to do things for them rather than teach them eventually to do these things for themselves.

There are, therefore, many advantages of learning, in a group, about entitlements and the rules covering them. Worked examples can be done, discussion occurs and knowledge is shared. Individual experiences often serve as useful knowledge to others who might find themselves in similar situations. Achieving an understanding of the welfare rights system in this context is a step forward in gaining confidence to negotiate with those who apply the rules. The HMI report says this of welfare rights classes:

The Inadequacy of the Current Situation

> The reality of the circumstances, the discipline of detailed analysis, and the ultimate need for interpretation and judgement provide an educational process of considerable potential.[37]

In the light of remarks like this, it is unfortunate to say the least, that much more of this kind of financial education does not take place.

Surviving financially within the present system of rules and regulations, learning how to make the most of a limited income and cope with debts, is clearly essential. However, if this is the extent of what is possible for those members of society who are denied access to paid work, then there can never be a chance for them to share in the 'good life' experienced by others. Therefore, some providers of education for unemployed people have attempted to encourage debates about the issues surrounding unemployment - its causes and consequences, the various theories and opinions about 'what should be done', and the actions which might be taken to improve unemployed people's situation.

The HMI report on the WEA says, 'A small number of courses could be said to make a direct approach to the task of improving the present situation of unemployed adults or seeking novel ways out of that condition.'[38] It goes on, however, to criticise the one day school observed :

> Another group undertook the apparently sophisticated task of studying possible alternative ways of organising employment, with emphasis on producers' cooperatives. The small group included two YTS trainees and one retired miner, with a part-time tutor who provided continuity for a series of visiting speakers. The group was serious and attentive but it was hard to see how the chosen content and method could be effective in meeting the diverse educational requirements of the members.[39]

In spite of criticisms such as these, this example is one of the relatively few overall. The Open University survey found that neither local education authorities nor universities nor polytechnics apparently addressed these issues in their provision aimed at adults who are unemployed. It would appear

The Inadequacy of the Current Situation

that the WEA is on its own in this respect. Issues such as 'the right to work', 'the obligation to work', 'the right to an income regardless of having a job or not', 'how wealth should be distributed' or 'who should have the jobs that are available?' do not figure largely in the content of programmes specially designed for unemployed people - or if they do, they are not mentioned.

This brings the discussion back to the first of the three overall aims stated at the start of the chapter - that any educational provision should take account of the different perspectives of the 'problem'. So what about the view that full-employment will never come back, at least in the sense that we have known it in the past? What about those perspectives that argue for changes in the way work generally is organised and shared among members of society?

EDUCATION AS SOCIAL CHANGE: A SEARCH FOR ALTERNATIVES

It is somewhat difficult to discuss existing educational initiatives which address issues such as the changing meaning of work and what sort of future is available to people who are unlikely to be needed to do full-time paid jobs, let alone how others may view this, because there appear to be hardly any. What there is seems to be the prerogative of the Workers Educational Association among the 'official' providers of education. Possibly, these issues are debated within other contexts - subject based classes or those concerned with local and other issues. Even then, this type of provision does not figure largely within that tailored specially to meet the needs of unemployed adults. Obviously, unemployed people can and do take part in such discussions outside the "enclaves" reserved solely for them. It is probable, however, that given the tendency to reduce social contacts and spend much more time in the home, this would not be great.

Critics of this type of provision would say that unemployed people themselves are not interested in examining the reasons for the unemployment of themselves and others and the prospects for the future. Survival in the present, it is argued, is their overwhelming priority. There is certainly some truth in this. Political debate and concern about

The Inadequacy of the Current Situation

the nature of society and its future is not of overwhelming interest to most people in the UK. Unemployed people, however, do stand to lose most if the status quo prevails. Certainly, other groups (e.g. women and ethnic minorities) who feel they are discriminated against within society, are now involving themselves in educational processes to improve their position. So why not unemployed people? The consequence of continuing to ignore the possibilities that there might have to be other futures than the 'employment' one must be serious, leading to even greater divisions in society with all that that could entail.

In the light of the above remarks, there would appear to be either an inability or an unwillingness on the part of educators to provide learning programmes which challenge the work ethic or concepts like 'the right to work' and 'the obligation to work'. By design or default there is an avoidance of discussion of the implications of continuing high levels of unemployment and the issues surrounding the future of work.

John Hughes writes:

> The post-war, repectably social-democratic, view held that publicly provided education should respect both individual need for development and social needs. The latter were not only directed at the acquisition of skills and expertise relevant to a mature economy, but also at a 'common curriculum', a shared experience........In sharp contrast, the last ten years have seen a persistent worsening of the combined poverty/inequality problem in all its connections with educational systems. The 'background' of social, and especially labour market, conditions has deteriorated to a staggering extent. And instead of educational resources being reinforced to offer some compensation for the massive enlargement of poverty and deprivation, we have witnessed repeated curtailment of educational finance and an often conscious pursuit of inequality.[40]

These may seem harsh words - others would point to the large sums of money being spent by the MSC on the Adult Training Programme in order to eliminate the 'mismatch of skills' problem. But, John Hughes is scathing about what he terms the 'mythology' of

The Inadequacy of the Current Situation

mismatch in a situation of vast unemployment. Referring particularly to the problem of youth unemployment, he says, 'This is not **mismatch** but social tragedy'.[41] In addition, he castigates the educational system for 'projecting the social myth that the problem is located within the unemployed themselves.'[42] The same is true for adults.

But, what about unemployed people themselves? How do they stand in this debate? The Birmingham Unemployed Resource Network which is in touch with and links together hundreds of centres for unemployed adults as well as other groups small and large, says in its magazine:

> The education system is another area in which some radical re-thinking needs to be given to the issues of unemployment. Educationalists tend to pride themselves on knowing what is wanted and the right way to present what they have to offer. These beliefs are at best untested, and at worst simply arrogant.....One lesson they might take to heart from the beginning is that the education and training we want may have no clear or direct link with market needs and future employment.[43]

These are brave words, and reflect the fact that this particular organisation is not constrained in what it can say or do by its sponsors or the source of its funding. Many unemployment centres, community groups, voluntary organisations and other informal groupings of unemployed people are held hostage to what they can do or say by those who supply the funds to keep them going. Evidence of activities which can be construed as 'political' can and does result in financial support being withdrawn. Even so, they are probably more willing to address the social and political implications of different explanations of unemployment and what can be done about it, even though they sometimes walk tightropes whilst doing so.

A multitude of factors appear to mitigate against widening the discussion about work and its place in society. The training perspective espoused by many politicians and the MSC excludes this possibility. Education in its wider sense, wherever it takes place has been shown to be limited, for as McDonald argues:

The Inadequacy of the Current Situation

> ....However, it is not intended to suggest that, even with the far-reaching efforts that have been made to serve the unemployed, the pattern of provision is sufficiently flexible to cater adequately for all their educational needs. On the contrary, the attempt to accommodate mature unemployed people within the existing framework has served to draw attention to its inadequacies and to the irrelevance of many of the basic assumptions on which it rests......It is necessary to develop educational strategies by which learning is more closely related to adult experience and the concept of continuing education given greater reality in practice.[44]

The Birmingham Unemployed Resources Network article referred to above concludes with the statement, '....it is now absolutely essential to open up the debate about alternative lifestyles in this society.'[45] If this can be done, then educational provision will indeed encompass a range of assumptions about the future and be reflecting needs of the majority of unemployed people. Thus, given the present and proposed provision in other fields described in this chapter, the first two of our general aims might be achieved. The degree of achievement, however, will be limited and incidental in many cases to the main thrusts of educational programmes towards satisfying the needs of employer-clients.

UNEMPLOYED PEOPLE AS INDIVIDUALS

Much of this chapter has been concerned with the 'content' of education for adults who are unemployed, that is, whether it is relevant to their needs and whether it addresses a wide range of political and social issues. Just as important, however, is how and where and when these people can take part in learning experiences. We must consider how educational opportunities compare with our third general aim, the response to unemployed people as individuals with needs which are specific to themselves, their families and their communities. This brings up the issue of choice and being able to exercise that choice. However, choice can only be

The Inadequacy of the Current Situation

exercised if the options are available and these options are kown.

In 1982, the ACACE carried out a survey of the educational experience and needs of adults.[46] This found that the majority of people were not able to suggest who arranges courses in their area. Those who did claim to know, listed :- local education authorities (20%), further education college/tertiary college (15%), and evening institute/adult education centre (13%). Even when prompted, of the sample of 1196 men and 1252 women, less than 14% mentioned university extra-mural/polytechnic continuting education departments, the Open University, community centres, women's institutes, sports centres, WEA, Government or trade unions. As expected, those judged to be from the higher social classes were much more aware of what was available than those from lower social classes.

The limited degree of awareness of educational provision is reflected in the low participation rates of adults generally in Adult and Continuing Education. 80% of respondents had not taken part in any course in the last three years. A survey of provision in the North West of England,[47] indicates participation rates for local education authority institutions as 3.5% in adult education centres and 2.6% in colleges.

These quite low levels of awareness and participation of adults generally in education, do not inspire optimism that unemployed adults are participating to any significant extent in education. This is borne out by the Northern Ireland survey which says,

> Respondents were asked to indicate whether they knew anything about local educational facilities and activities. This reveals that almost 80% do not know anything about these activities and facilities.......Those over 50 years of age are most likely not to know about such facilities or to require more information about them. The youngest age groups are the most likely to require further information.[48]

Another survey on the educational needs of 116 long-term unemployed adults in both urban and rural districts of Scotland states:

The Inadequacy of the Current Situation

> Seventy one respondents had no current learning contacts, yet had unmet 'needs to know'. When it came to assessing which sources could <u>actually</u> help them, few of this group were able to be certain. Only six felt confident that they had identified the appropriate targets.[49]

Even if sources of educational provision are known, many factors can work against people taking part. The way that much of education is organised does not really relate to the patterns of unemployed people's lives. 'In one authority it was admitted that the concentration of much of the non-vocational adult education into evening programmes in the technical college had an adverse effect on enrolments by some sections of the community.'[50] The requirements of fixed terms, enrolments, numbers needed to make up a class, fees and receipts are important to maintain operational efficiency and suit those whose lives change according to the calendar and the clock. Yet they mitigate against the involvement of unemployed people, for whom there are no days off, shifts, holidays and so on. For those lacking in confidence, depressed and having low psychological and physical energy, large institutions, centrally located in impressive buildings can be intimidating. Siting local adult education classes in secondary schools during the evenings is also not the answer. And although unemployed people are accommodated in other places - unemployment centres, church halls, community centres and other 'non-educational' places, the scale and nature of this kind of provision, goes nowhere near to fulfilling the requirement of the third of the aims specified earlier.

In short, the standard pattern of educational timetables and locations does not fit with the different time perspectives and mobility of unemployed people. Neither can it be claimed that the majority of responses are meeting the requirement of being 'wide ranging, flexible and accessible'. Programmes and courses tailored to the personal needs of large numbers of students pose a challenge to the educational system. The existence of external goals in terms of qualifications or job opportunities provide a convenient framework for course design and legitimate methods of teaching and learning. Where goals are internal to each participant, the process will have to include a

The Inadequacy of the Current Situation

continuing renegotiation of the learning contract between the student participant and the teacher facilitator. It is clear that such arrangements are rarely available at the present time.

CONCLUSIONS

It has become clear that most of the provision being made for those who are unemployed is prescribed and unidimensional in aim, that is it is directed towards immediate or eventual employment. This is not to decry the efforts of those educationists who are devoting their energies to raising the level of many unemployed people's basic skills so as to enhance their quality of life or enable them to participate in more advanced education. However, limited resources, problems of access and the constraints of a 'coping strategies' framework, mean that participation rates are low and restricted to a small minority of the total number of adults who have no jobs. The fact that much of the effort is through Type I and Type III agencies raises the question of fundamental differences between the traditions of these agencies and the needs of participants. Also, this type of provision has little to offer the increasing number of adults, who, though unemployed, have perfectly adequate skills of this kind.

There is a singular lack of education which aims to help individuals and groups to influence events which shape their lives and to search for alternatives to a social organisation one of whose basic values is full employment, in other words to bring about community and social change.

The 'problem', therefore, which now confronts all those who believe that learning helps the achievement of individual potential as well as being the means to social progress, is how education for unemployed adults should be defined and organised.

NOTES

1. Barbara Senior, 'Adult Educational Responses to Unemployment', <u>Adult Education, Vol.57, No.3,</u> (December 1984), pp. 228-237
2. Open University survey, see Chapter three

The Inadequacy of the Current Situation

3. HMSO, _Training for Jobs_, Her Majesty's Stationary Office, Cmnd. 9135, London, (January 1984)
4. Ibid., para. 41
5. Joan McDonald, _Education for Unemployed Adults: Problems and Good Practice_, Department of Education and Science, (October 1984)
6. Op.cit. p.1
7. See Chapter three
8. Op.cit. p. 12
9. Ibid.
10. Op.cit. p.12
11. Conall Boyle, 'Time to Pull Out - And What Then?', _NATFHE Journal_, Number 8, (December 1984)
12. Ibid. p.37
13. Op.cit. p.5
14. Ibid.
15. Ibid.
16. John and Sue Munday, _What the Unemployed Want?_, The New University of Ulster Institute of Continuing Education, (24th August 1982)
17. Op.cit. p.3
18. Ibid. p.35
19. W.W.Daniel, _The Unemployed Flow_, Policy Studies Institute, (May, 1981)
20. Ibid. p.IX.1
21. Ibid. p.IX.2
22. Op.cit. p.4
23. Op.cit. p.IX.5
24. Wider Opportunities Courses (including Wider Opportunities for Women)
25. Op.cit.
26. Lord Young, at the time Minister without Portfolio and former Chairman of the Manpower Services Commission, quoted in _The Guardian Newspaper_, (26th January, 1985), p.3
27. Senior, op.cit, p.233
28. John Hughes, 'The Inequality of Impoverished Education', _Poverty, Child Poverty Action Group Journal,_ No 58, p.20, (August, 1984)
29. Report on the 'Continuing Education and Training for the Long-term Unemployed, CEDEFOP Conference, Berlin, 7-9 March, 1984', in _Adult Education, Vol 57, No 1_, (1984), pp.74-75
30. Bryan Nicholson, 'Focus on Adult Training', _MSC Press Notice_, (20 November 1984)
31. Op.cit.
32. Ibid. p.24
33. Op.cit.

The Inadequacy of the Current Situation

34. McDonald, op.cit. p.21
35. J. Dixon, R.W. Grainger (University of Durham) & J. Lawton (South Tyneside LEA), *Account of the Genesis and Progress of Work with the Unemployed in South Tyneside*, (1984)
36. Department of Education and Science, *Report by HM Inspectors on Workers Educational Association Provision for Unemployed Adults*, DES, (1984)
37. Ibid. p.7
38. Op.cit. p.10
39. Ibid.
40. Op.cit. pp.19-20.
41. Op.cit. p.21.
42. Ibid.
43. David Hopson, 'Dialogue with the Deaf', *The BURN Magazine*, (1984) pp.6-7
44. Joan McDonald, op.cit. p.36
45. Op.cit. p.7
46. Advisory Council for Adult and Continuing Education, *Adults: Their Educational Experience and Needs*, ACACE, Leicester, (1982)
47. Keith Percy, Stephen Butters, John Powell, and Irene Willett, *Post Initial Education in the North West of England: A Survey of Provision*, ACACE, Leicester, (1983)
48. Northern Ireland Council for Continuing Education, *The Educational Needs of Unemployed Adults*, NICCE, (1983) pp.25-26
49. Ian Bryant, *The Educational Needs of Long-Term Unemployed Adults*, monograph, Department of Adult and Continuing Education, University of Glasgow, (October 1982) p.71
50. Joan McDonald, op.cit. p.10

CHAPTER FIVE

TOWARDS A RE-DEFINITION OF EDUCATION FOR UNEMPLOYED ADULTS

In the light of our critique of educational provision for unemployed adults, it would be easy to conclude that unemployment is too large and complex a problem for educators to do other than provide narrowly focused courses related only or mainly to the concept of 'employability'.

This may well be true, especially if the commitment to the modern work ethic continues to hold. For example, at a conference of adult educators held under the auspices of one of the Further Education Regional Advisory Councils,[1] it was stated that professional educators might have very little to offer unemployed people within a work-ethic frame of reference. Others have pointed out the difficulties inherent in the formal systems of education in doing much that relates to the needs and lifestyles of those people who have been unemployed for many months and even years.

The situation can be complex and confusing. To wait for trends to emerge, for society to change, is an easy response. This is the reflective view of education. Educators have neither the vision, nor the ability, and some would also say not even the right, to attempt to lead society into new territory. Yet, in relation to questions such as the role of women and the position of minorities, pioneering educational programmes at all levels have been applauded. The education system could equally well clarify issues and take a lead in the redefinition of the relationships between work and employment, joblessness and low status.

Three things must be done. Firstly, there must

Towards a Re-definition of Education for Unemployed

be a continuing challenging to, indeed an attack upon, the modern interpretation of the work ethic itself. Secondly, new thinking about the needs of unemployed people is required to express them in terms of learning rather than education and training. Thirdly, there must be a greater emphasis on understanding the personal position of each unemployed person as a pre-requisite for educational choice and action.

CHALLENGING THE WORK ETHIC

So far we have referred to the work ethic as a sort of sticking point, something that if it were removed there would be a realignment in society and a resolution of many of the problems of unemployment. The work ethic vaguely accounts for, and justifies, the notions of role, job and related status and income.

The education system relates to and reinforces the present day role-job-status-income structure. If blame is to be apportioned, then education must bear a large share. Increasingly, initial career development has moved out of employers' concerns into educational institutions. Craft and commercial apprenticeships, articles and technical training have been replaced by college courses from craft certificates to sandwich degrees. A consequence of this change is the rising power of education as it controls the key to entry to many careers.

The status structures within the adult and continuing education system reflect the world with which it has a symbiotic relationship. Community colleges and universities each see a role for themselves and jealously guard their positions. Students develop concepts about the nature and usefulness of courses in relation to these roles. Institutions generally present their courses as means to an end, the end being enhanced prospects in the job market.

We have shown already how closely status is related to job and how the work ethic has come to mean that all have the right to a job on a more or less permanent basis. The obligation to work and, indeed, the right to work have become such dominant values that it is difficult for us to imagine a situation when things were different. Yet the development of policies to sustain full employment

Towards a Re-definition of Education for Unemployed

is a relatively new phenomenon and the periods during which unemployment has been very low form brief interludes in our history.

We showed in chapter two how employment, where incomes are dependent upon the labour market, is a product of the urban industrial society. Unemployment was a normal part of life before industrialisation and high unemployment has characterised much of the period since. Indeed, in spite of commitments to full employment which began to be made by governments around the period of the first world war, the UK has barely enjoyed one generation of its occurrence in practice. A concept and commitment that can be learned and adopted so quickly could be equally quickly unlearned and abandoned. Unemployment changed, in about 1914, from being a social problem to an economic problem. It is equally possible to change once again.

The need is pressing. Krishan Kumar[2] shows how the wage-market system simultaneously reinforced and destabilised employment. The job market was created at the same time as technological progress was reducing the need for jobs. This process has accelerated and now applies to industrial manufacturing, service and administration. Firms are in business to make profits and not create jobs. Expansion of businesses often occurs with little expansion of labour forces.

In maintaining a general commitment towards career education, institutions and governments take the easy way out. School teachers try, with rising difficulty, to offer the promise of a good job as a reward for effort. Increasingly, the opposite is recognised. As one WEA organiser said, 'Now that the institutions of education and employment can neither predict nor guarantee the access to employment and wages, we enter a new game.'[3] But, as long as having a job continues to be seen as the gateway to status and respectability - the only real way to express one's identity - then education for other purposes than to increase employability will remain marginal and something to be experimented with. Such education will not be taken seriously by those in control or properly resourced.

With full employment a short term phenomenon in our history it is remarkable how it has gained such a powerful hold in the social and political mind. There must be a questioning, a challenge to the modern interpretation of the work ethic. Being

Towards a Re-definition of Education for Unemployed

unemployed is unlikely to be the fault of those who find themselves without jobs.

Removal of the negative association of unemployment would be a considerable advance and some[4] say that we should get rid of the concept of the work-ethic altogether. So, instead of unemployment continuing to be viewed as something negative, defined in terms of what people did not have, a job, with its attendant status and income, it could be thought of in terms of being 'free from work'. This, then, opens up the possibility, for those who have time, to choose learning for its own sake, or to go further and learn to take action to enhance the quality of life for themselves, their community and ultimately society.

Challenging the work ethic in this way has, of course, certain consequences for the content of learning. There can no longer be an avoidance of the political aspects of policies concerning jobs and those who do or do not have them. Concentrating on one particular view will no longer suffice. Education for all who are interested in these issues, but particularly for those most directly affected, must involve an examination of the whole spectrum of opinions about the causes and consequences of different policies and practices. Continuing to emphasise a single perspective must be seen as inadequate.

Challenging the work ethic must also have implications for the role of education, not just in what is taught, but in terms of what constitutes learning. This means an examination of the concepts of 'teacher' and 'taught'. In other words, a re-definition of what has generally come to be accepted as 'education', and, in this context, education appropriate for an adult population having to cope with the problems of the present and the possibilities of many different kinds of futures.

EDUCATION, TEACHERS AND LEARNERS

Webster's Complete Dictionary of the English Language (authorized and unabridged edition of 1880) defines 'education' as:

> The act or process of educating; the result of educating, in knowledge, skill, or discipline of character, acquired; also, the act or

Towards a Re-definition of Education for Unemployed

> process of training by prescribed or customary course of study or discipline.[5]

The synonyms of 'educate' are given as :

> To instruct; teach; inform; breed; bring up; train; mature; rear; discipline; indoctrinate.[6]

Moving into the present century, this definition can be compared with that given by the 1970 edition of Cassell's English Dictionary:

> education..... The process of educating, systematic training and development of the intellectual and moral faculties; instruction; a course of instruction; the result of a systematic course of training and instruction.[7]

More up-to-date still, the 1979 edition of Collins Dictionary of the English Language gives:

> ...the act or process of acquiring knowledge, esp. systematically during childhood and adolescence....the knowledge or training acquired by this process....the act or process of imparting knowledge to, esp. at a school, college, or university....the theory of teaching and learning...a particular kind of instruction or training.[8]

A hundred years have done nothing much to change the definition, that seems clear. 'Prescribed', 'customary', 'systematic', courses of study, training, and instruction still predominate. The last definition goes even further to associate education particularly with formal teaching institutions. Given this focus on training, instruction, and systematic courses, (even though discipline and indoctrination may not now be fashionable) taking place within formal institutions, it seems entirely reasonable that, in the context of the present discussion regarding adults in particular, the concept of education thus defined, might well be a candidate for retirement.

A ray of light may be perceived, however, in debates about the roles of 'adult education' and 'community education'. Tom Lovett et al[9], use terms such as 'permanent', 'recurrent', 'continuing', 'life-long', which they say are used to signify a

Towards a Re-definition of Education for Unemployed

new concept of adult education to meet the challenge of the latter part of the 20th Century. Teachers may pose as tutors, advisers, coordinators and facilitators. They go on to say, though, that reorganising adult education to emphasise 'client's needs', 'co-ordination of resources', 'effective delivery of services', may result in more institutionalisation and bureaucratisation. For example, good teachers have always attempted to respond to 'client's needs' through adaptation of the curriculum and personal interaction. Adopting such responsiveness as an organisational goal may lead to the development of bureaucratic processes to implement and control adaptations to clients' formally expressed needs. Therefore, care must be taken to ensure the existence of strong community control.

Unfortunately, institutionalisation or not, other pressures are now being applied to post school education including the adult and community sectors. There is pressure to reverse the trends described above, through applying market place values to the concept of education. Lindsay Martin quotes from a piece written by the Head of a Department of adults studies in a further education college:

> Colleagues who just a while ago were carrying out community development work have shaved off their beards, changed their jeans and sweaters for grey flannel suits and set off to marketing our expertise to local businessmen.

The reversion back to the tradition of packaging education in predetermined ways, is being encouraged by the policies of the Manpower Services Commission. These are to 'buy' courses for those in and out of employment. These are then 'applied' to those considered suitable. So unemployed people are expected to go through programmes of study - in at one end, out at the other - suitably remodelled to await their turn in the employment (or unemployment) queue.

Lindsay Martin goes on to talk about the philosophical pressure from government:

> ....a shift of provision to a more instrumental, geared-to-the-needs-of industry/commerce type which survives (or not) according to the laws of the market -place

Towards a Re-definition of Education for Unemployed

(student numbers, student:staff ratios, etc.). It is a move away from provision which is conceived to be educationally important for its own sake rather than merely financially viable.'[11]

Education for adults who have no jobs and little hope of getting one has no meaning if used in this way. Concern is sometimes expressed about 'keying people into the educational system'. What is required, even more than ever now, is that the system should be keyed into what people need and want. This means abolishing the distinctions between liberal education, functional education, recreation and training. It means playing down education and emphasising learning.

FOCUS ON LEARNING

Stressing the idea of 'learning' rather than education is not merely playing with words. Firstly, in relation to the people involved, it moves the focus from those who provide to those for whom the provision is made - from the teachers to the learners. It takes us from the passive to the active. The notion of teaching conjures up images of 'students' and 'being taught', wheareas focusing on learning implies active participation on the part of those involved.

The idea of 'student-centred learning' has been around for a long time. The proposal here is that learning should be people-centred. This means that it is not only teachers who can teach and students who can learn. Walter James said,[12] 'Wherever there is action there is learning' and so teachers might or might not be part of the action. If this is the case, what about the methods used and the form that learning should take?

Without a doubt, most people learn by doing, and particularly so when they have control over and are responsible for their own actions. John Traxler, Chair of the National Federation of Voluntary Literacy Schemes, says '...if education is about enabling people to have more control over their lives then those people ought in all honesty, to be able to control their education.'[13] In circumstances where 'you belong to the state, you are run by the state',[14] it is crucial that unemployed people, experiencing the negative mental

Towards a Re-definition of Education for Unemployed

and physical effects of their situation, should, through whatever means possible, increase the amount of influence they have to affect that situation. So, what form can people centred learning take in relation to adults who have no jobs, and as a result are in the main living impoverished existences?

Lindsay Martin[15] identifies two kinds of educational provision which she argues are important. The first she refers to as the '"liberal education" taught-class provision as embodied in the extra-mural tradition',[16] - the desire for learning for 'its own sake'. The second is based on a community education/development model with its emphasis on the group rather than on the individual. To these two, can be added a third - 'incidental learning', and a fourth - 'education for capability'. All four kinds of provision are relevant to the needs of unemployed people. These are now discussed.

Learning For Its Own Sake

The notion of learning for its own sake is certainly relevant to unemployed people who may choose to spend their enforced leisure in some form of learning which is related purely to their interests and curiosities and which they do not see as in any way functional to their particular situation. The adult education services as presently structured do make some provision for these needs. Difficulties arise, however, in meeting the requirements of those people in our society who are not restricted through work commitments and 'holidays' to classes in the evenings and during 'term-times', even if they know they existed in the first place. Unemployed people can and want to learn throughout the year and, in particular, during the day time.

Many years ago, as a teacher of dressmaking and tailoring, one of the authors used to travel from village to village responding to requests for classes from groups of residents in the different places. Often the people requesting the class would find the place where we could meet. Having a car enabled necessary equipment like a sewing machine, iron and ironing board to be brought along.

The classes were formed in response to requests by the people in the locality and the author, like so many other part-time temporary employees of the local adult education service, was available to meet these requirements - indeed, because many teachers

Towards a Re-definition of Education for Unemployed

were only available on a part-time basis, these arrangements suited them all. The classes were held mornings or afternoons on days to suit the learners, who were of 'mixed ability'. The needs of the individual participants as expressed by and agreed with them took precedence over most things. The only constraint on the classes was their duration - two hour 'slots', and that they were restricted to term times - and so 'suspended' three times a year to match the arrangements under which most formal education falls. Of course, the system, to work, relied on the people in the villages knowing how to activate it.

This mode of learning has much to recommend it in relation to the needs of unemployed adults. With more variable patterns of attendance - every day for a week; evenings throughout the summer; afternoons in winter; weekends in spring - and the large body of part-time, temporary, willingly peripatetic 'teachers' - learning interventions could happen anywhere and anyhow.

For unemployed people this is important. However, like those requesting dressmaking classes, they must be able to 'activate' systems to benefit themselves and not least those which encourage learning. They might do this if the systems were brought to them, rather than expecting them to find them out for themselves. For instance, there could be provision within unemployment benefit offices to encourage people to chat about what form of learning could be of use to them. Some 'quick response system' could then make available what was required at a time and place to suit the requesters. If desirable, this might be in people's own homes. Adult education in this context becomes the servant of the learners. The 'teacher' intervenes as the people at the receiving end choose. The group 'employs' the teacher.

Learning for its own sake, though posed here as mainly learning for interest, merges in many ways into learning because of the 'need to know'. Unemployed people are at the sharp end of the effects of the new technologies which reduce work tasks. They, more than most, have to learn to cope with economic and organisational changes; but they, weighed down by the penalties society puts upon them, are, more than most people, least able to do this.

Towards a Re-definition of Education for Unemployed

They should be able to use education to acquire skills and to use it instrumentally to help them in their day to day living and management of their affairs. Those who are unemployed need to enlarge their knowledge and range of abilities to do things which will advantage them.

In everyday life much of what we need to know is got 'incidentally', through contacts at work, with friends and relations, the media and so on. For unemployed people, these contacts are frequently reduced. Not only is a person likely to meet with a narrower range of people but he or she is not likely to be joining with them in purposeful activity in which learning can take place. So, this kind of learning, so suited to the 'need to know' type of learning, should be included in any redefinition of education for those who are unemployed.

Incidental Learning

Roger Cann says, 'Adult educators in Britain have an unnatural appetite for classes and getting people into groups in their centres.'[17] He goes on to say, '...but there is also incidental learning, where relevant information is gained outside any curricula setting'.[18]

Incidental learning goes on during coffee breaks, waiting for the 'teacher' to arrive, on train journeys and so on. Basically, one or more persons are telling one or more others something of the 'I know where...I know how...I know about...' kind. This kind of giving and receiving of knowlege, opinions, and skills is so important to many people yet so unrecognised. Educators could establish means by which the lost opportunities caused by unemployment are replaced and improved upon. In such ways a chain reaction could occur with new learners passing on their knowledge in turn to others. And it does not necessarily require professional educators to do this.

Take the group of people attending a benefit office during any day, and you will find they have between them a range of knowledge and skills, let alone varying opinions about things which, if shared, could benefit themselves and others. If opportunities can be given for these people 'to test their knowledge and abilities against others in a supportive environment, then incidental learning can create great personal satisfaction and contribute significantly to changes in attitudes and perceptions.'[19] It is unlikely, however, that the best setting for this is within the environment of a formal classroom. Alternative more amenable places are pubs, cafes, community centres, people's houses, benefit offices themselves, common rooms in factories and clubs.

Examples of incidental learning (one of which is discussed in detail in the next chapter), can be found in the context of groups of unemployed people meeting in one of the numerous unemployment centres now operating on a self-help basis. For unemployed people, perhaps depressed and low in confidence, to be able, with support, to tell others what they know, share experiences and perhaps change someone else's opinions, is a powerful tool in creating new confidence and the will to try to change their situation.

The opportunities available within any self-help initiative to involve members in organisation and administration are all examples of incidental learning which can be built upon to become semi-structured learning experiences. Those who are unemployed can be an instrument of learning for others. Roger Cann[20] recommends bursting apart the structures of adult education to provide greater opportunities for this kind of shared learning. Without the constraints of fees, timetables, and registers, much could be done in this direction.

Incidental learning can, then, contribute significantly to personal development through learning for its own sake and the need to know. In addition it can provide a springboard for group and community action. However, knowledge and how to do things may not be enough on their own to lift unemployed people out of the severely disadvantaged position they now find themselves in.

An article[21] in the publication 'Work & Society' asks why there has been no single powerful campaign on behalf of the unemployed, despite the fact that about four million are unemployed themselves, with several times that number affected indirectly. One of the main reasons put forward is the lack of crucial skills among unemployed people. About these skills the article says, '...both the skills, of organisation and communication, and the confidence to believe that campaigning can be effective, are often lacking.'[22] So, unemployed people need to become more competent in planning and organising as well as more able to cope with

Towards a Re-definition of Education for Unemployed

changing circumstances. They must develop their creative abilities, not only to help themselves, but also to co-operate with others to become the producers of change, not the victims of it. In short, they must increase the range of their abilities.

Capability Through Learning

> There is a serious imbalance in Britain today in the full process which is described by the two words 'education' and 'training'.[23]

Thus begins the manifesto of the Royal Society of Arts 'Education for Capability' scheme. The imbalance referred to is one of too much emphasis on two aspects of education, namely 'comprehension' and 'cultivation' - that is acquiring and recording specialised knowledge and learning to appreciate the values inherent in our cultural heritage. The manifesto goes on to say that the imbalance is harmful to individuals, industry and society. What is missing is 'the exercise of creative skills, the competence to undertake and complete tasks and the ability to cope with everyday life: and also doing all these things in co-operation with others'.

The capabilities of **competence, coping, creativity,** and **co-operation** are important to all people. As already noted above, however, they are especially important to people who are unemployed and in particular if their situation of unemployment persists. It is within the world of work that many of these qualities are developed, practised and tested. For many people, having their job taken away from them, has the effect of undermining their confidence in themselves as competent, coping human beings. Opportunities within employment may not always be there to develop creative abilities, but within the sterile existence of much of unemployment, there are often none at all. In addition, the social isolation experienced by many unemployed people - adults in particular - reduces the number of ways to help and be helped - that is to co-operate with others.

So, regardless of the content of learning, importance must be attached to increasing people's capability not only to assemble data about things and analyse what they have found out, but to

Towards a Re-definition of Education for Unemployed

formulate problems, create and organise solutions, in particular through joining with others.

In the literature of organisational psychology, mention is made of two types of leaders or managers. The first of these are those who are mainly concerned with the task, whose drive is to get the task done. The others are those who are more concerned with the people who carry out the tasks and how they can best operate. Bales and Slater called these two types of leaders 'task-orientated' leaders and 'socio-emotional orientated' leaders.[24]

The first of these can be likened to teachers of 'subjects' - traditional teaching concerned with imparting knowledge. The second are more akin to those who use experiential forms of teaching - role playing and games. Emphasising the learning of processes, as required in learning for capability, necessitates a different style of teaching to that where identified knowledge or practical skills must be imparted. Educators involved with this kind of learning will have to act more like agitators, animateurs, facilitators and coordinators. Yet most educators are trained to 'teach' - 'take a class'. They are often regarded as 'experts' who can tell students what they need to know and do. Much teaching is prescriptive and to be fair, many students expect it to be so.

It is often beneficial, therefore, to play down the role of educator and enhance the role of co-ordinator. As an example, a skilled co-ordinator in a centre for unemployed adults can, with some resources, facilitate learning where the users of the centre plan what they need to learn, organise the resources required to put their plan into action, and take responsibility for its outcome. By doing this they will at the same time be developing their creative abilities, learning to cope with whatever arises to frustrate their intentions and show competence and co-operation.

Being 'capable' is a quality which benefits the individual in his or her pursuits. It is also, as the Work & Society article indicates, necessary for the pursuit of any collective action. This is still not enough, though. Individuals may change their ideas, attitudes and behaviour, but are unlikely to act together to change their social situation unless they first of all feel a sense of community and appreciate the effects that different social

Towards a Re-definition of Education for Unemployed

structures have upon them. So, any re-definition of education for unemployed people must also include aspects of what is known as community education with its focus on issues rather than subjects.

Community Education
The concept that something is 'wrong' with the condition of unemployed people and there needs to be a 'cure' continues to dominate education policy making. For example, at the meeting of the Further Education Regional Advisory Council referred to at the beginning of the chapter, one of the discussion group considered what the content of provision for unemployed adults should be. The suggestions given were:

> * Developing and augmenting vocational and general skills
> * Helping individuals cope with their changed situation
> * Developing intellectual, creative and physical abilities.

All these are contained within those aspects of learning discussed in this chapter up to now. They are all important. However, they do emphasise only the needs and cure concept. There is a neglect of any mention of education for social change, based on the possibility of increasing awareness of the processes whereby individuals come to be unemployed. There is no reference to the need for those who are unemployed being given the means to influence the system which affects them so greatly and which they seem powerless to do much about.

Re-defining education for unemployed people means not only finding more effective ways of developing individuals' abilities and their intellectual and practical skills, but enabling them to act collectively to bring about change in themselves, their situation and their society. Thus, unemployed people need the opportunity to 'talk through the changing patterns, definitions and values of work, recreation, unemployment and enforced leisure....It is crucial (for them) to engage in the debate that looks at socially responsible work, novel forms of industrial organisation (e.g. work-sharing, worker co-operatives) and the socially equitable distribution of resources.'[25] It is also crucial

Towards a Re-definition of Education for Unemployed

that, having engaged in the debate, they can find some way of taking action, and be supported in this by educators and others.

This is more easily said than done. Most people in this country do not deliberately gather together to discuss economic and social systems over which they feel to have no control. For many the concepts are too abstract, the information too immense and the learning skills too underdeveloped. Voting every now and again in local and national elections is about the extent to which most people feel they should get involved. Becoming unemployed does not necessarily reverse this inclination. Yet becoming unemployed does certainly sharpen the awareness of those affected of the inequalities built into a social structure based on employment. Dissatisfaction is endemic among unemployed people. The desire for change is strong yet the feeling is one of hopelessness.

For these people, community education is one means of sharing their experiences in their lives and communities with others of like situation with the possibility of action resulting to change that situation. Community education by definition concerns itself with matters important to members of a community. It is important, however, that those who seek to facilitate learning for community action understand the relationships between approaches and consequences.

There are several different approaches to community education.[26] All of them take education into the community. Some of them focus on the personal development of community members in the hope that this will have spin offs for the community as a whole. Others put more focus on local action with adult educators 'working in local communities in a variety of community projects providing information, resources, advice and, when the occasion arises, opportunities for more systematic learning and training in specific skills and techniques relevant to such action.'[27]

A third puts greater stress on linking community education to community action in the belief that community action is in itself an educational process. Instrumental education may be provided, but the emphasis is particularly on political education. A fourth is based on an approach which assumes a more formal and demanding educational effort on the part of the participants.

Towards a Re-definition of Education for Unemployed

The focus is on social rather than community action. Education is more structured based on a belief that through education the origins of local community problems will be perceived as being located in the larger social, economic and political structures in society.

All these approaches, grounded in educational practices involving people in mainly working class residential areas, are relevant to those who have no jobs. However, it is the last two which, though requiring significant effort on the part of educators, offer the opportunity for unemployed people to raise their eyes above the day to day details of surviving to focus on wider issues and how these might be resolved. Learning in this context should include learning how to involve those who are employed, as well as those who are not, in the issues of work in the community and larger society. This is more easily accomplished within a community when it can be tied to direct action.

Learning is not always easy and unemployed people do not automatically turn to educators to solve their problems. Lovett says, 'One cannot expect positive results from an educational or political action programme which fails to respect the particular view of the world held by people'.[28] So, educators must first take their time to learn from those they would 'help' by listening and talking and acting with them in their daily endeavours. Only then may they 'know' what needs to be done. Finally, it must be realised that 'social and political education requires time, effort, patience and sensitivity, that it is no overnight process but one demanding long term commitment and resources'.[29]

UNDERSTANDING SELF AND SITUATION

Almost every time we have asked those working to help unemployed people what educational provision for them might be like, the one thing they say should not be dwelt upon is talking about what it is like to be unemployed. They stress that it is more important to get those who are unemployed to 'look forwards not backwards', to 'take positive attitudes to themselves and their situation', and to do something constructive like getting a hobby or retraining for 'something new'. Yet almost every time

Towards a Re-definition of Education for Unemployed

we have been in discussion with groups which included unemployed people the talk has been predominantly about just that.

Chapter one discussed, in some detail, the psychological effects of being unemployed. It is not intended, therefore to reiterate that here. The danger, however, is for those who are not affected by unemployment in this way to recognise these effects but then ignore them. There is sometimes a conspiracy of silence on the assumption that if ignored they might go away. Those who complain about their circumstances and how they feel are sometimes labelled as 'pathetic', 'inadequate', 'without moral fibre'. The educator is anxious to say, 'Now we have discussed unemployment, let's get on with the business in hand.'

However, ignoring the feelings of these people and the effects their unemployment has on their family and life in general, is no answer. Stephen Murgatroyd and Ray Wolfe describe quite clearly how the loss of a job is a traumatic experience for most people and the emotional effect is often akin to that resulting from the death of a relative or friend.[30] Many people who become unemployed go through 'grieving' periods in just the same way as those who 'lose' a loved person for whatever reason - death, separation, divorce. Unless this grief is allowed expression, and unless individuals are given the facilities to work through their own particular situation, any moves forward relating to individual or collective action are unlikely to occur.

What unemployed people need is , 'a rediscovery of personal worth, confidence and a willingness to act - whether politically or educationally - a refusal to acquiese in powerlessness, apathy and demoralisation. The challenge is to create more experiences of such quality for a wider range of people'.[31]

CONCLUSION

The title of this chapter, 'Towards a re-definition of education for unemployed adults', was deliberately phrased so as to avoid any definitive prescription, if one could be found. Unemployed people are individuals with unique needs and desires, yet they have many of these in common as well. Occupying a disadvantaged position in our

Towards a Re-definition of Education for Unemployed

society, the suggestions here are that whilst, in the short term, they must have access to tools with which they can cope with their situation better (and these, of necessity, have to be made accessible), this should not obscure the fact that unemployment is a social, economic and political problem.

Concentration on short-term responses allows the continuance of an acceptance of the modern interpretation of the work ethic. Enabling people merely to survive within this framework is in itself unsatisfactory. There must be a prospect of change, a reason for hope.

We have seen how much educational provision has been based on hope either of an immediate job or training 'for stock'. Yet participation rates in training among unemployed people are low and they have begun to learn that prospects are not substantially improved by this type of activity. The more people participate in the conventional programme the more they will perceive its futility and the more they will seek change.

The dominant values surrounding the modern work ethic stultify efforts to find imaginative, unconventional responses to unemployment. The challenge to the education system lies in three directions. Firstly, there is the unravelling of the complex relationships which form our society, the role and status systems, the myth of full employment, the legitimation of government action by this myth. Unravelling and understanding these can then lead to the creation of alternatives. Secondly, there is the questioning of what education and educators are about. The control of the content and context of learning should be in the hands of learners as clients as much as teachers as providers. The changes that this implies may range from increased student power on management bodies through to a redefinition of the activities which take place in classrooms and other settings.

Thirdly, and finally, there is the need for learning to begin from the situation of where people are, in their emotional state and practical circumstances, to squarely facing the expectations people bring with them to learning, to recognise what they think education can give them and to discuss its limitations as well as opportunities. The next chapter describes a number of initiatives taken by and for unemployed people which illustrate some of the proposals put forward here.

Towards a Re-definition of Education for Unemployed

NOTES

1. Meeting in Ipswich in Febrary 1985, organised by the <u>East Anglia Regional Advisory Council</u>.
2. Krishan Kumar, 'Unemployment as a Problem in the Development of Industrial Societies: the English Experience', <u>British Journal of Sociology</u>, Volume 32, Number 2, (1984) p.218
3. Greg Wilkinson, <u>WEA Unemployed Report: Progress Report</u>, WEA Swindon Area Office, (16 March, 1984).
4. Op.cit. Suggestions made at the Ipswich meeting of the East Anglia Regional Advisory Council
5. <u>Webster's Complete Dictionary of the English Language</u>, George Bell & Sons, London (1880) p.429
6. Ibid.
7. <u>Cassell's English Dictionary</u>, Cassell, London (1970) p.360
8. <u>Collins Dictionary of the English Language</u>, William Collins Sons & Co. Ltd., (1979), p.466
9. Tom Lovett, Chris Clarke, and Avila Kilmurray, <u>Adult Education and Community Action</u>, Croom Helm, London, (1983)
10. Lindsay Martin, <u>REPLAN and the Future of Adult Education</u>, National Association of Educational Guidance Services, Occasional Publication No.5, (1985), p.11.
11. Ibid.
12. Walter James, <u>Developments in Adult Education - Community Perspectives in Europe</u>, Paper given to the Southern Regional Council for Further Education (Advisory Committee for Adult and Continuing Education) at East Hampstead College on 25th February, 1985
13. Written in a letter, dated 29th October, 1982, to Professor Brian Groombridge, Department of Extr-Mural Studies, University of London
14. Comment by an unemployed person, reported in an article, 'The Morning After, Back on Desolation Row', <u>The Guardian</u>, (28 March, 1985)
15. Op. cit.
16. Ibid. p.12
17. Roger J. Cann, 'Incidental Learning', <u>Adult Education</u>, Volume 57, Number 1, (1984) p.47
18. Ibid.
19. Ibid.
20. Ibid.

21. 'Campaigning among the Unemployed', an article based on infomation and discussion with Jim Radford who has been closely involved with the National Unemployed Workers Movement, Work & Society, number 7, (January 1985)
22. Ibid.
23. Taken from the manifesto of 'Education for Capability' sponsored by the Royal Society of Arts, London
24. R.F.K.Bales and P.E.Slater, 'Role Differentiation in Small Decision-making Groups', in T.Parsons, and R.F.Bales, (eds) Family, Socialization and Interaction Process, The Free Press, New York, (1950)
25. National Federation of Voluntary Literacy Schemes, Cambridge House, 131 Camberwell Road, London SE5, Evidence presented to the Advisory Council for Adult and Continuing Education on The Educational Needs of the Adult Unemployed, (December 1981)
26. Lovett et al., op.cit.
27. Ibid. p.37
28. Ibid. p.72
29. Ibid. p.83
30. Stephen Murgatroyd and Ray Wolfe, Coping with crisis, Harper & Row, London (1982), see chapter 9 in particular
31. Linden West, 'A Response to the MSC's "Towards an Adult Training Strategy - A Discussion Paper", April 1983', Appendix One to Adult Education and Unemployed People, Report of a workshop held on 14th May, 1983, WEA Berks Bucks & Oxon

Chapter Six

UNEMPLOYMENT INITIATIVES AS LEARNING EXPERIENCES

This chapter describes a number of self-help initiatives taken by or for unemployed adults. The authors directed a number of action research projects during the period 1979 to 1985 and these examples have been selected both because they represent a range of types of educational provision described in chapter three and illustrate some of the arguments made in the last chapter. Two of the examples are similar in that they are based around the concept of a skills exchange, yet in other ways they differ considerably. The third example is a set of small co-operatives using a community development model to generate employment opportunities. In each case learning took place in a variety of ways to bring short term relief to unemployed members and also to explore possibilities for the long term.

The drawback of using a few examples is that they can illustrate only a narrow range of possibilities and, of the many feasible relationships between the key elements of providers, users, stakeholders, management and mode of learning, only a few are explored. Understanding in depth, on the other hand, enables one to consider issues of application of models to reality, to see how real life does not fit into regular categories and how initiatives can be functional at more than one level. Thus it will be seen that the labelling of an initiative as, say, a 'skills exchange' should not cause one to search merely for utilitarian benefits and purposes through an evaluation of tasks carried out. It may be that wider and deeper benefits, in educational and other terms, are

Unemployment Initiatives as Learning Experiences

available to participants and may indeed be perceived by them as being more important.

Hence our case studies, temporary, even ephemeral in nature and grounded in the opportunities and traditions of particular communities, are intended to create an awareness that much can be achieved and much needs to be discovered.

MANOR EMPLOYMENT PROJECT

Manor Employment Project (MEP), started in 1981 by taking over a disused light industrial site in the Manor Estate area of Sheffield. Funded by the Employment Department of Sheffield City Council, the project enables groups of Manor residents to set up small business enterprises committed to the principles of co-operation. MEP's stated aim is:

> To encourage, assist and be engaged in the establishment of businesses and other opportunities, primarily through co-operative and community-owned enterprises, with a view to training residents in particular skills, providing them with work, and assisting them in making new employment.
>
> The Project aims to show that, with the right kind of assistance, working people who are supposedly "unskilled" can take control of their own futures and can, through mutual aid, create viable alternatives to unemployment or low-paid work for others. MEP is concerned that it be as accessible as possible to Manor residents who have not previously been encouraged to take initiatives.
>
> In particular the Project is concerned to provide for women usually tied at home and unable to work "normal" working hours and who have had to take manual part-time work, if that.

Manor is a large, pre-war, overspill estate. With many of the 4000 houses having structural faults and standing empty awaiting the progress of the repair programme, the area has an air of despondency. Unemployment is high.

Unemployment Initiatives as Learning Experiences

MEP has four main buildings on a two and a half acre site. These are divided up into units suitable for workshops, offices, a canteen and nursery. A small management staff (development worker, site manager, administrative assistant) run the site and give assistance to the individual enterprises operating on it. These include three people carrying out car valeting, a group of six women involved in a dressmaking co-operative, one man and an apprentice who produce wrought iron work and steel fabrications, two women who run the canteen as a co-operative, a man who works part-time operating the renovated weighbridge which is on the site, two small enterprises set up by unemployed engineers and metal workers on the one hand and an electrician on the other, a photographic workshop and an office cleaning co-operative.

Each person in each of the individual enterprises is a member of MEP itself and can attend the monthly General Meetings at which all policy decisions regarding the site and all its enterprises are taken. Typical items on the agenda of such meetings are applications from individuals and groups to join MEP, grants or loans of money from MEP to any of the enterprises, matters such as site security, the nursery facilities and so on. All members of MEP have a vote at the General Meetings.

Individual enterprises are organised mainly on co-operative lines and depend heavily on all the people involved for their success. Thus members bear heavy responsibilities not only for the productive work of their firm, but also for its organisation and management. In this they are coached by the development worker through his role in their business meetings. He also holds weekly site surgeries where problems can be discussed and advice received. Where necessary, a training programme is worked out in relation to the business tasks. Where appropriate, training can be carried out through the Adult Education Department of the City Council.

Many of the businesses have been started by people who had previously been employed making the same product line. The opportunities for them to start up on their own arose from the collapse of former employers' businesses. At the other extreme there are enterprises starting from scratch.

Silver Needles is a remarkable example. This dress-making co-operative was formed by a group of women who had no experience of the trade. Six

Unemployment Initiatives as Learning Experiences

members worked for two years without pay learning how to design, purchase, make and sell. MEP was able to offer administrative aid, advice on organisation and connections with a local college, one of whose fashion design students assisted greatly in developing the product range.

MEP Membership as a Learning Experience

In terms of achieving control over their lives through increasing their confidence as well as their capabilities in a great number of directions, the learning gained through participating in MEP is effective. When asked to compare MEP with conventional employment, members of MEP are unanimous in endorsing their preference for MEP. This is so, even though many do not draw wages for months and even years.

MEP is an unemployment initiative which is attempting to find genuine alternative life styles for its members. It is committed to developing people's personal and business skills and involving them fully, not only in the management of their own enterprises but also in the management of MEP. Many of MEP's enterprises, however, remain frail and could not trade independently without the support of the Project itself. What MEP has shown, however, is that unemployed people can learn the skills of business organisation and know also how an organisation to help others gain these same skills can and does operate. They understand that, if other unemployed people like themselves are to get their chance of changing their lives and situations, new structures such as MEP might be needed.

During our research period, we noted time and again the critical role of the development worker. With the project reaching 50 members on site, about half of whom were engaged in businesses which could be considered 'viable', the development worker found that his resources were fully stretched. Members recognised the value of training and saw that success depended heavily on this being made available. The MEP pamphlet, in its comment on the future says, 'Some provision for specific education/training programmes is another priority, in particular devising ways in which adult education resources can be imported to the Manor in order to provide a more accessible service which is flexible and able to respond to specific local needs'.[2]

Unemployment Initiatives as Learning Experiences

MEP is an example of a conventional response to the problems of unemployment. Grounded in principles of self-help and co-operation and backed by good grants from charitable trusts and the local authority, its main aim was job creation. Members wanted, perhaps, different types of jobs but they certainly wanted jobs.

The educational value of the project was evidenced by the great changes that took place in the members. Not only did many develop and learn practical skills but they also learned interpersonal skills from effective use of the telephone through to chairing a general meeting. Education was informal, often incidental, yet the way in which it was closely tied to needs meant that it was highly effective.

TIT FOR TAT

Whereas MEP was not primarily an education project, we have shown how much of its activity can be seen as educational, particularly in training terms. In contrast, the Adult Learning Project set out to improve people's lives through education. We were invited to study one group within ALP, Tit for Tat. This skills exchange project had interesting features because of its relationship with its parent organisation, hence ALP will be described first.

The Adult Learning Project
ALP began in 1979 after Lothian Regional Council obtained sponsorship for the project under the urban aid programme. Three full-time community education workers were given the task of developing community-based informal adult education in Dalry-Gorgie, Edinburgh. ALP has shown how a valuable project can be developed from scratch using a particular educational philosophy.

The process which ALP follows is:[3]
(1) An initial investigation by full-time staff with local volunteer participants, aimed at identifying key <u>themes</u> and <u>concerns</u> of people living and /or working in the locality.
(2) <u>Codification of themes</u> - usually this has meant taking photographs or making drawings of <u>important social situations</u>, such as mothers gathering on the pavement outside the gate of the primary school; sitting in the local baby clinic; children playing

Unemployment Initiatives as Learning Experiences

in the street amongst parked cars; workers streaming out of the gates of Ferranti; Scottish men celebrating victory on the pitch at Wembley; and so on.

(3) <u>Decoding discussions</u> - led by a <u>co-ordinator</u>, who is either a full-time worker or a local trainee. Groups of local people respond to these pictures in their own way, analysing the meaning for them of the situations represented.

(4) At each stage, workers and local participants <u>summarise</u> their discussions, and out of these summaries emerges the full <u>education programme</u>, a series of courses integrating <u>"saying your own word"</u> with the use of outside tutors to present <u>new knowledge</u>, shedding light on the themes and issues identified by participants at previous stages. Such programmes have included courses on The Family Today; You and the School; On Being Scottish; Women and Well-being; and Unemployment and Health.

(5) The final stage is the <u>action stage</u>. Education is not seen as leading only to greater understanding, but also to action to improve the situation. Examples of local <u>action spin-offs</u> from ALP education programmes have included:- Play in the Terraces; the Skills Exchange; the Well-Woman Centre; the Writers Workshop; Church House Groups; the Welfare Rights Group; and the Living Memory Project. In this stage, local people take over as co-ordinators/leaders of their own groups, with training sessions organised for them by the ALP full-time workers.

From this description of the ALP philosophy and method of facilitating learning within educationally disadvantaged groups, it can be seen that such a process with its emphasis on people's own experiences and action is entirely in line with the re-definition of education for unemployed adults discussed in the previous chapter. Tit for Tat, referred to in the final stage as the Skills Exchange is one of the outcomes of this process. The following describes Tit for Tat and the way that this particular 'action spin-off' from the ALP educational process incorporates learning in its organisation and activities.[4]

Tit for Tat
Tit for Tat emerged in 1981 from the activities of the Adult Learning Project. One of the Tit for Tat

Unemployment Initiatives as Learning Experiences

newsletters describes the beginning of the project as follows:

> In October 1981 a small group of women in ALP were discussing people's dependence on paid employment and the effect of redundancy on families, including their own. They wanted to do something practical about the waste of people's skills and experience, and the fact that low incomes make it impossible to pay to have essential jobs done. They hit on the idea of a skills exchange.
>
> Because the idea of a skills exchange had emerged from an ALP programme, Tit for Tat began life with a ready-made base in the ALP Shop. Joan, the ALP secretary is available during the day to answer all initial enquiries about the Exchange, maintain the register of new members and put members in touch with one another.[5]

A skills exchange is set up to match members' offers, in terms of skills and time, with wants, in terms of jobs that they are unable to do themselves. Members receive practical benefits. There is also potential for social and psychological satisfaction from being able to do useful work for others. Various systems of accounting for jobs done are possible[6] ranging from direct equivalent exchange to those based on ideas of reasonable give and take. Tit for Tat chose the latter.

Although not exclusively for unemployed people, at least half of Tit for Tat's members do not have jobs. Membership of the group is in the region of 70 of whom 7 on average attend the weekly members' meetings with an average of 15 attending the monthly meetings.

The administration and meetings of Tit for Tat take place within the ALP premises. These consist of a pleasantly converted corner shop with office facilities and sitting area where meetings, discussion groups and other activities take place. Tit for Tat only involves members collectively once a week at the business meetings and once a month at the social meetings. This does not, however, preclude members visiting the shop at any other time and indeed they are required to do so to find out

Unemployment Initiatives as Learning Experiences

who might be available to do a job for them when this is needed.

Gerry Kirkwood, the ALP worker having responsibility for Tit for Tat, continues in the newsletter quoted above:

> In the first fifteen months, as ALP worker with responsibility for Tit for Tat, I attended all meetings and had a leading role in co-ordinating the core group of active members who ran the exchange. Members dropped in to the ALP shop on Friday afternoon, set the exchanges in motion, talked over problems and dreamt up new ideas for development. But only a few members were willing or able to take an active part in organising the Exchange and we quickly realised there was a danger that Tit for Tat would become like every other community organisation, run by a few for the benefit of the many. This seemed to go against the basic principle of mutuality of give-and-take which is at the heart of the Exchange.[7]

The result of this thinking was that in the spring of 1983, a new "deal" was struck with ALP. In return for the resources which ALP could supply (paper and postage, secretarial services), Tit for Tat would become more independent, organising itself through a rota of volunteers. From this time until the beginning of 1984, this volunteer system involved members who took responsibility as co-ordinators for a month at a time. Each was assisted by another member who was, as it were, in the role of "trainee". The assistant moved into the role of co-ordinator at the end of the month. The co-ordinator and assistant were supported by a rota of other members who attended the weekly meetings and helped with tasks such as producing the monthly newsletter, keeping the files, meeting visitors, arranging learning exchanges and socials.

Early on in the development of Tit for Tat, the weekly meetings were reserved for administration and day to day running with the monthly meetings concentrating on bigger policy issues and reflecting on its progress. Eventually, the weekly meetings took on both these aspects, the monthly meetings being mainly social with demonstrations of skills by one or more of the members. Sometimes, outside people come to talk about their activities or

Unemployment Initiatives as Learning Experiences

interests. From time to time, however, the ALP worker intervenes at the monthly meetings with a session which encourages members to reflect on their experiences in Tit for Tat and its activities.

Members of Tit for Tat are regularly encouraged to review their roles and commitments and the progress of Tit for Tat in relation to its philosophy which is firmly based on the concept of mutual help rather than charity. Lesley Cunningham, a member, comments on this:

> Tit for Tat is not a "charity" and we have always felt that it is vital to stick to our original idea of "give and take" and to insist that <u>everyone</u> has something to offer. We don't believe that the world is divided into two - people who do things and people who have things done for them - and so, if someone asks for help, we usually try to persuade them to join.[8]

Everyone who joins Tit for Tat is expected to contribute to its organisation and operation. Merely taking part in exchange is not considered enough. Gerry Kirkwood reminds members:

> Indeed, when your name appears at the top of the rota list you will get a phone call reminding you that it's your turn to attend meetings for a month, as part of the deal involved in being a member.[9]

Retaining members and fully involving them in the life of Tit for Tat is considered important. So a system of 'key' members has been instituted to assist in this process. The district has been divided up into eight areas each with a key member. This member has information about other members in the area and is responsible for encouraging them to be active in Tit for Tat. Delivering newsletters personally to members enables the key member to say when the next meeting is and how welcome a person will be if he/she comes along.

Exchanges are the core activity of Tit for Tat. These determine and legitimate the other processes. In common with other skills exchanges, there is a surplus of offers over wants and the encouragement of members to ask for a job to be done is an important activity.

Unemployment Initiatives as Learning Experiences

Tit for Tat as Learning Opportunity

Tit for Tat is one of a range of initiatives which have been called Skills-LEAP (Skills and learning employment alternatives projects)[10]. Tit for Tat was partly modelled on an earlier skills exchange, The Network, which we discuss below. Yet it has its own identity based on an explicit commitment to an educational process. This is clearly the influence of its 'parent' organisation, the Adult Learning Project. The skills and ethos of the community education workers at ALP have resulted in deliberate learning opportunities being constructed.

Firstly, the ALP worker has throughout been involved in 'tutoring' the co-ordinators and others concerned with the organisation of Tit for Tat. In one twelve month period 8 members acted as co-ordinator with as many others editing the newsletter. From time to time, during members' weekly and monthly meetings, we have observed the subtle but gentle influence of the ALP worker in sensitively directing the process of organising and decision making. This is again a reflection of an educational ethos with the ALP worker seeing herself as facilitating learning without wishing to direct the particular outcomes in terms of content. Examples are encouraging the group to learn from situations which have been difficult in some way or making opportunities for a hesitant member to participate.

So, members learn how to control their own organisation and take well thought out steps to assist its development. Many comments in the newsletter and by members when interviewed testify to the increased confidence in their own abilities gained through taking responsibilities in this way. The probability of success for these individuals is increased by the tutoring they receive.

Secondly, learning opportunities for Tit for Tat members come also from their using each other as resources. The co-ordinators 'teach' the assistants how to cope when their turn comes. People write pieces for the newsletter and then become editor in their turn. There has been far more emphasis on learning exchanges in Tit for Tat, than in other skills exchanges with which we are familiar. So, as well as "doing things for each other", members share with other individuals or groups their particular skill.

Unemployment Initiatives as Learning Experiences

Examples are one member teaching another a language and the tapestry and weaving workshop led by one member in her own home, interspersed with watching 'Dallas' on television. An imaginative innovation was to negotiate with a local Youth Training Scheme to have the weaving frames made by youngsters learning carpentry and joinery. The emphasis on learning has been brought into focus by holding an open day for members of the public demonstrating the possible learning groups which could be formed.

Learning exchanges within Tit for Tat resemble closely the developments in incidental learning described by Roger Cann. He outlines the process of 'brainstorming' he used to identify from his group what interests and special topics they wanted to learn about, following this up by asking members who had suggested topics to present them and lead a discussion. In the case of Tit for Tat, possibilities for learning exchanges are obtained from the list of offers of skills supplied by members. Members are approached to see if they are willing to 'teach' others and favourable responses are then publicised.

A third way in which learning is incorporated into Tit for Tat lies in the deliberate effort on the part of the ALP worker to engage the members of Tit for Tat in a process of 'reflection on action'. This has meant their being 'forced' to stop every so often and consider where they are and where they are going. They have been learning to review not only their activities but also the philosophy underlying them. Such a process could form the basis of reviewing not just their individual commitment to a particular way of expressing mutual help, but the implications of this for their community life and the wider society.

To the present, Tit for Tat has not explicitly linked the activities and development of the skills exchange with an exploration of the underlying socio-economic reasons for unemployment. Without a deliberate input involving some attention to the social and political implications of attempting to change the attitudes and behaviour of unemployed people, it is unlikely to go much beyond the remit of 'mutual exchange'. However, many Tit for Tat members do go on to involve themselves in other programmes supported by ALP as well as those elsewhere.

Unemployment Initiatives as Learning Experiences

From the end of 1983 onwards, as happens inevitably with almost all 'experimental' initiatives, the end of ALP's funding was in sight. Since then, the effort required to secure continuation of its existence (with only two full-time workers rather than three) has taken its toll on its ability to support its individual projects. During this time, Tit for Tat has explored a number of ways it could become, itself, independent of ALP, none of which have been successful. The immediate future of Tit for Tat depends on the continuing support that ALP may be able to give it, although there is talk of it being taken out of ALP and, whilst maintaining the concept of skills and learning exchange, being developed to incorporate voluntary work with movements into forms of paid work.

The potential of an organisation developing from straightforward skills exchange to learning exchanges to forms of co-operative self employment on a part-time or full-time basis is discussed more fully in 'Skills-LEAP'.[12] This will not happen, however, unless significant learning as defined in chapter five can be facilitated.

THE NETWORK

It has been mentioned that Tit for Tat was modelled on an earlier project set up in Liverpool. While there is a risk of overemphasising skills exchanges as learning opportunities, it is useful to consider another example because of its contrasting philosophy and outcomes.

The Network operated from 1979 to 1983 in the centre of Liverpool under the auspices of the Merseyside Council for Voluntary Service. Its relatively long survival was underpinned by substantial grants from a charitable trust and the ability to use comfortable rooms, office equipment and, eventually, a workshop. Membership was open to all although most were unemployed and few were under 21.

From the start the founder members of The Network felt that they wanted to challenge existing employment structures and societal arrangements. They expressed this in terms of the need 'to find practical solutions to the problems of rewarding work'.[13] They felt that:

Unemployment Initiatives as Learning Experiences

> a resource exchange had the potential to provide the non-economic functions of employment and that successful operation would lead to changed attitudes in the wider society towards work, the unemployed, and welfare benefits.'14

Although the concept of 'exchange' was embedded in the thinking underlying the Network's foundation, the giving and receiving of skills and time did not necessarily take place on a reciprocal basis. All jobs done by members for each other were on the basis of 'reasonable give and take'. So, there existed a 'pool' of offers from which members drew according to their needs, and into which they gave as they could. No money exchanged hands, it was neither given nor taken - the only method of accounting was a loosely defined one of a job for a job. If the carrying out of a job incurred expenses, these were paid for by the recipient.

Members' meetings were held weekly and all were welcome. The position of chairperson and secretary were rotated among those attending with all decision making being by consensus. The meetings often took up a good deal of time with arguments for and against policies being strongly made. Suggestions for how to spend the grants made to the organisation were also made at these meetings.

Members carried out administration, that is arranging exchanges, publicity, organising group activities and social events, and producing the newsletter. Two or three, who committed themseves to being in the office more than the others, were designated 'full-time members'. These members occupied their roles for three or four months and, though volunteering for the task, still had to have the support of the members' meeting. Office work counted as if a job had been done for another member. Thus, credits for jobs done could be accumulated in this way.

During the three years involvement of the research team with the Network, the number of people who could be counted as members fluctuated, but was on average 130. Even so, 191 members were counted as having done at least one of the total number of 469 exchanges. The exchange activity was, however, concentrated among some 15 of the members.

The Network survived as a skills exchange for nearly four years until the sponsorship money ran out. The Merseyside Council for Voluntary Service, the 'umbrella' organisation, then decided to move away from its commitment to skills exchange to one involving the setting up of projects under the Community Projects Programme of the MSC.

The Network as a Learning Experience
The Network did not have within its stated aims an overt commitment to education or learning. Interestingly, however, the results of structured interviews with 60 members showed that the need for The Network to provide for 'learning and knowledge' was considered more important than other needs such as social, autonomy, achievement and self-esteem.[15] Even when the more active members' responses were separated from the others the same result was found.[16]

A skills exchange organisation such as The Network, though having no formal educational input, is nevertheless, a good example of how effective learning can happen. The environment in which the Network was set up - with one of the staff of MCVS acting as facilitator and adviser and committed to the concept of democratic decision making and organisation - was helpful to the type of incidental learning which it is argued should be an integral part of any educational provision for unemployed adults.

Members were encouraged and 'coached' in their roles as chairpersons and secretaries of the members' meetings. It was found that hardly any of them had participated previously in this kind of situation at all, let alone acted as chair or taken minutes as a secretary. The skills exchange enabled members to exercise and maintain existing skills. Eventually a workshop enabled more explicit learning opportunities to be available, where some members could share skills with others.

In the involvement of members in decision making, administration and the doing of jobs for others, each individual was increasing his or her capabilities. A number of 'group exchanges', that is several Network members doing a job for outside organisations in return for something of value to the Network as a whole, required co-operation and members had to learn how to resolve conflict.

There were problems from time to time. Members' meetings were not always models of democratic decision making and tempers were sometimes short.

Unemployment Initiatives as Learning Experiences

New members attending some of the meetings must have wondered what they were letting themselves in for. Induction procedures were patchy, although they improved when a full-time paid coordinator was appointed after some 18 months. There needed to be more reflecting on people's experience, particularly newcomers who tended to get swamped with the telling of the history of Network and 'how it is and and has always been'.

Observation of the organisation and activities of The Network led to the conclusion that a more explicit teaching/learning intervention could have brought many benefits. For example, when the workshop was completed, its full potential was never realised through lack of any structured initiative involving either members acting as teachers to others, or the engagement of 'expert' help. The members' meeting never quite gained control over the direction and policies of the organisation or their own actions within it. Democratic structures notwithstanding, the strong personality of the person within MCVS who was one of those who originally conceived the idea of a skills exchange, and hence had proprietorial rights, tended to dominate some of the decisions. His role was reinforced by the position of MCVS as 'banker' and his responsibility to ensure that correct accounting procedures were maintained. With this expert and position power, MCVS was able to control and constrain policy making particularly by declaring that certain actions would be ultra vires.

Above all, there were not built into The Network mechanisms for individuals to locate themselves within a wider community, and so become more aware of their situation within the larger social system. The Network remained, throughout its life, rather inward looking. Most discussions were about the group itself and only occasionally about its relationships with other institutions. When members were asked what aspects of the Network's structures and procedures were most important, they rated 'organisational growth and development' as being one of the highest. Yet when asked how satisfied they were with this, they rated it the lowest.[17]

There is a problem here. A number of members were strongly committed to the idea of alternative life styles. They had become cynical about many of the education providers. This meant that links with agencies, particularly those of Type II, which could have been fruitful were never made. Isolation was not just a result of rigidity or suspicion on the part of providers but also a choice made by group members themselves. The ability of the Network to link its members to wider goals and purposes was very limited.

The Network skills exchange was, in spite of the limitations referred to above, remarkable in the way many of its members used and developed their skills and abilities and extended their experience of organisation and management. The potential for learning in such an organisation is great. Within The Network, a significant proportion of this potential was realised. However, a more structured series of interventions by educational facilitators, in collaboration with the 'members, would have enabled learning to extend further into the lives of the individuals involved. In addition, it could have begun a process of raising awareness of the larger forces affecting unemployed people's lives in particular, and how these might be influenced.

CONCLUSION

The three case studies illustrate ways in which initiatives can bring both short term relief and pose a long term challenge. In each case those interviewed reported that their lives had been improved by membership. There were considerable social and psychological benefits from participation and members were learning from each other how to cope with unemployment.

MEP had a strong training orientation which suggests that it might be seen as a Type III, Training Programme provider. Yet its stakeholders and providers were not employers and training contractors but the members themselves using the resources of a number of sympathetic organisations.

Tit for Tat, sponsored by a local education authority, was beginning to pose a long term challenge to the question of unemployment. Learning was taking place very much for its own sake, much of it was informal and incidental and there were the beginnings of community education on the isssue of unemployment. Nominally a Type I initiative, Tit for Tat was gradually taking on the characteristics of a Type IV, community development agency.

Unemployment Initiatives as Learning Experiences

The Network set out to challenge the work ethic and its consequences. In many ways it resembled a Type II, participating member agency project. Members of The Network, as a community, learnt a great deal from each other yet it was not a community project in the sense that it did not find a way to persuade others that alternatives were available.

None of the examples fits easily into the classification of Chapter three. This suggests that successful innovation may need to be preceded by a breakdown of conventional relationships between providers, users, management, stakeholders and mode of learning.

NOTES

1. <u>Manor Employment Project</u>, pamphlet produced by MEP describing the nature of the project and its constituent enterprises, (1983-84)
2. Ibid.
3. 'The Adult Learning Project in Dalry-Gorgie - A proposal for the future', (24 September 1984)
4. The description of Tit for Tat is based on research carried out by the EARG during the 12 months to December 1983. This involved one of the research team spending time every week with the Tit for Tat group, interviewing members and observing all members' meetings. The results of this research have not yet been published, but any further information can be obtained from the authors
5. Gerry Kirkwood, 'Tit for Tat - Next Move?', <u>Tit for Tat Newsletter</u>, (Nov/December, 1983)
6. Barbara Senior and John B. Naylor, 'A Skills Exchange for Unemployed People', <u>Human Relations</u>, Vol. 37, No. 8, (1984)
7. Op.cit.
8. Lesley Cunningham, 'Tit for Tat and Other Organisations', <u>Tit for Tat Newsletter</u>, (March 1983)
9. Op.cit.
10. Barbara Senior, 'Skills-LEAP a palliative or an alternative to employment and unemployment', <u>BPS Occupational Psychology Newsletter, Number 16</u>, (August 1984)
11. Roger J. Cann, 'Incidental Learning', <u>Adult Education</u>, (February 1984)
12. Senior, op.cit.

13. MCVS *The Network: a Mutual Exchange of Time and Skills*, pamphlet, Merseyside Council for Voluntary Service
3. Ibid.
14. Senior and Naylor, op.cit.
15. Ibid:
16. Barbara Senior, 'Evaluation of Member Satisfaction in a Skills Exchange for Unemployed People', *The New Psychologist*, (January, 1983)
17. Senior and Naylor, op. cit.

Chapter Seven

DISTANCE TEACHING AND SELF-PACED LEARNING

The results of the survey of educational provision described in Chapter three and the examples of learning given in the previous chapter present something of a paradox in relation to educational provision for unemployed adults. On the one hand, formal institutions like the MSC are able to deliver large amounts of money for employment related training even though serious doubts still remain as to whether jobs will be available at the end of that training. On the other hand, we find that a project such as the Adult Learning Project has had to put much of its effort over a period of fifteen months to securing resources for its medium term future. Again the Manor Employment Project in Sheffield virtually relies on one person to provide or arrange for educational and training inputs.

It is clear that some parts of the formal systems are well funded, albeit for particular prescribed purposes. On the other hand more informal, perhaps more imaginative, and it could be argued more useful initiatives, have to rely on short term grants scraped together with great effort from this, that or the other source Even when it may appear that some longer term security is becoming available such as in the recent, and overdue, REPLAN initiative, we find that much of the money will go on curriculum and staff development, planning and co-ordinating with a relatively small proportion being spent on direct provision.

It is to the credit of people concerned with the whole range of learning needs of those without jobs, that they have achieved as much as they have

Distance Teaching and Self-Paced Learning

with such few resources. As Linden West, a district secretary with the WEA puts it:

> 'Change', unemployment, redundancy do not simply produce or result from 'manpower' problems or skill obsolescence but intermesh with personal upheaval, low levels of self-confidence, negative self-images and a loss of faith in any ability to influence the course of events. ...This tension between the extent of "change" and limited educational resources is considered to be central to our current social and economic malaise.[2]

What is required is some way of extending the limited educational resources which are available to unemployed people. Such extension should enable our general aims to be achieved more effectively. Particular difficulties are posed by the third aim, the appreciation of the individuality of unemployed people. The need is for provision which addresses them as intelligent, reasonable adults, who can exercise choice in relation to the content, form, time and place of their learning. Distance education which includes self-paced learning has traditionally been regarded as a means of offering choice and flexibility to learners. It has also had its detractors who would stress isolation, poor motivation and the second best nature of the learning experience. This chapter examines distance education to discover whether it offers possibilities for achieving our aims.

DISTANCE EDUCATION

Distance education occurs when the teacher and learner are separated, usually by space and time. More formally it is 'broadly equivalent to non-contiguous learning, in which the teaching and the learning occur separately, in contrast to contiguous learning where teaching and learning occur simultaneously'.[3]

There are many forms from correspondence courses and individualised tuition to self-help study groups. Distance education has been seen as one type of open learning system which opens up educational opportunities to those who do not

Distance Teaching and Self-Paced Learning

participate at the moment. A NIACE report gives the following characteristics of open learning,

* There will be minimal restrictions on time or place of study
* There will be no group size requirement
* There will be provision to help financially disadvantaged students meet the cost of study
* Where courses continue to have objectives chosen by agencies other than the student it will often be necessary to provide individualised "link" material to bring the student and course objectives in line, and bring student attainment to the necessary level
* There will be continuing efforts to remove or decrease restrictive aspects of assessment methods and course entry requirements.[4]

Although the last of these definitions is prescriptive in some detail, taken together all the definitions suggest a range of possibilities for distance teaching. Thus distance education varies from one-way non-interactive instruction (through print, audio, video etc.) to fully supported instruction supplied at a location which is nearer to the learner than the agency which produces and provides the materials. A variety of types (interaction through mail, telephone, teleconferencing, occasional tutorials) exist between these two.[5]

While it is clear that any combination of these methods could facilitate learning for unemployed people, they would not all be equally effective. Good distance learning should recognise the individuality of the learner, starting from the identification of the learner's present position and allowing him or her to plan and control the learning process. The content of the provision should be relevant to needs.

In the case of unemployed adults, we have emphasised problem of isolation and cynicism with respect to much of what education has to offer. Education for capability may be important but there are also needs for learning for its own sake and community education. In particular, the recognition of unemployment as a societal issue whose basis need to be understood and challenged in the long term is important.

Distance Teaching and Self-Paced Learning

Since this sort of education is not focused upon immediate instrumental objectives but is more concerned with coping in the long term, questions of motivation and relevance become important. Learners with, as has been stated, little educational experience, need support in order to make progress. This may be motivational, to replace the immediate instumental objectives, practical, to assist with using the learning materials or social, overcoming the isolation which is at first seen as a consequence of distance learning.

In the light of this it is unlikely that one-way, non-interactive instruction would be satisfactory. There must be interaction with, and support from, fellow students, teachers and others.

In the following sections two common types of distance education are examined to see how far they can go in meeting the educational needs of the unemployed.

Correspondence Courses

Correspondence courses can include print materials, audio and video tapes, games, photographic materials, models, experiment kits and so on. Most commonly available are printed materials which form 'correspondence texts'. These can be centrally produced by institutions such as the National Extension College, the Open University and independent correspondence colleges, or they can be prepared by staff in a traditional teaching institution such as a college or adult centre.

In the majority of cases, learners register with the institution concerned, and by studying mainly in their own homes, are formally assessed in their work by tutors appointed by the institution producing the materials. The aims, objectives and structure of the teaching materials are decided by the producing institutions and the students accept these when they register to take a course.

Printed materials are sometimes supported by the addition of radio and television programmes (particularly the case with centrally produced materials) or any of the elements mentioned above. Face-to-face tutorials have become a feature of some correspondence courses, the tutor mediating between the producing institution's intentions and the students interpretation of the materials.

Clearly, anyone who is unemployed could study a chosen subject using this method. The Open

Distance Teaching and Self-Paced Learning

University, a major distance teaching institution, spends £600,000 per annum to allow unemployed students to study for very reduced or no fees. The majority of this money is taken up by unemployed adults studying for a degree using the multi-media system of distance teaching for which the University is well known. The remainder is used for unemployed people taking shorter courses within the University's Continuing Education programme. Many of these and other courses can and do fulfil the desire for 'learning for its own sake', as well as providing learning for more instrumental reasons - because of a 'need to know'.

Some educationists argue, however, that correspondence courses are not appropriate for people who are unused to learning, who have few if any, educational qualifications and no experience of education since leaving school, characteristics of many unemployed people. In these circumstances, the negotiating of objectives with prospective students and the face-to-face element in teaching is said to be essential and paramount. It is further argued that distance learning is only a second best option for those who cannot regularly attend classes.

In response, it is clear that it is not always those who cannot get to conventional classes who study 'at a distance'. The ACACE report[6] gives two intrinsic reasons why some people prefer distance learning. Firstly, there is the flexibility of distance learning which allows learners to study at individually convenient times rather than having to adjust their study timetable to the requirements of the academic year. Secondly, there is the self-paced nature of distance learning with a preference for studying alone and wanting to avoid classrooms and schools.

Of course, self-pacing can mean a number of things. Study for a degree with the Open University allows self-pacing only in so far as students may study at any time of the day or night, but must submit assignments and attend examinations at specified dates. On the other hand, when taking one of the Open University short courses, for example one related to health or parenting, self-pacing means something much more flexible regarding times of study and return of assignments. In many cases dates are not specified at all.

In addition to the flexibility and self-pacing benefits, distance learning can have two other

Distance Teaching and Self-Paced Learning

beneficial aspects. These are not always found in the classroom. Firstly, studying at a distance helps the development of transferable skills - faster reading habits, critical faculties, logical analysis and selective note taking - quite apart from subject specific skills. Secondly, there is the 'accessibility of distance learning for diffident and educationally inexperienced adults who might be intimidated by participation in classes.'[7] This last point is supported both by tutors involved with students following correspondence courses, as well as by the students themselves, who recognise that 'the enhanced self-image and development of self-esteem was one benefit from distance learning which had a particular personal potency'.[8] This must be relevant to unemployed adults in the light of all that has been said about the social and psychological effects of unemployment.

This discussion of correspondence courses has mentioned the role of tutor from time to time. This role and the creation of study groups are important means by which learning can be made more available. Before discussing these, however, there is another open learning system not relying on prepared materials, which can be considered.

Individualised Study

This mode of study, though categorised as distance learning, does not rely primarily on prepared courses as such. Adults generally enrol at a college whose tutors then design a course to suit the individual needs of the particular learner. The course is a mixture of currently available distance teaching materials, directed reading, individually arranged exercises and possibly some means of assessment. In addition, the variety of courses, flexibility of attendance at tutorials and submission of assignments is likely to be greater than in other types of distance learning.

Obviously, it is not a requirement of individualised study that it be based on a college. Individualised study programmes can be devised by anyone not necessarily attached to an educational institution. It is, however, unlikely that such a programme would be effective unless the person devising it had the relevant skills to identify the learner's needs, know what learning materials are available, put together a coherent learning

Distance Teaching and Self-Paced Learning

programme and support the student throughout his/her studies.

Linden West, writing about the needs of unemployed adults, refers to the requirement to have learning programmes adjusted to a less frenetic pace, through individual support and through removing unnecessary 'testing'.[9] This is certainly possible with individualised study. Another advantage is that small resources can go further when existing distance teaching materials are used to help individuals in ways not possible within larger groups.

Individualised home study, coupled with tutorial and self-help study group support, can be a powerful method for facilitating learning among unemployed people. Through its ability to pace study according to individual and group needs, it can also incorporate into its plans space for any action based on what is learned.

It is more likely that action based on learning will occur where learners have the opportunity to come together in groups to discuss their individual reactions to learning materials and discuss what they might do as a result of their new knowledge. It has already been mentioned that there is increasing use of a face-to-face learning element in distance learning systems, hence the tendency to use the term open learning instead. Interactions with tutors usually take place in groups and the role of study groups will now be considered.

THE ROLE OF STUDY GROUPS

The limited research regarding the effectiveness of distance learning suggests that, as far as educationally inexperienced learners are concerned, participating in study groups helps to sustain learners' motivation as well as increase the value of the learning process.[10] The role of study groups within an open learning system can be illustrated by reference to those encouraged and organised by the Open University in relation to its wide ranging distance learning materials.

The Open University is set up to be a distance teaching institution in all its aspects. Thus, emphasis is on the correspondence materials which undergraduate and continuing education students receive. When the first undergraduate students were

Distance Teaching and Self-Paced Learning

admitted in 1971, the role of the tutor was very much that of a tutor in traditional higher education institutions. Involvement with the students was purely on an academic basis, personal study problems being dealt with separately by a counsellor.

By 1975 this split system of counselling and tutoring was considered to be inadequate and for first year courses the two roles were combined. New students are now assigned to a tutor-counsellor who acts as study advisor, academic tutor and assesses sudents written assignments. Staff at the University now realise that students need more than just good quality materials. As the intake of educationally inexperienced adults has increased, the role of the first year tutor-counsellor has become more important. First year students now have the opportunity of attending about eighteen tutorial and counselling sessions in the year, with a weeks residential school occurring in the summer. In addition to this, students can contact their tutor-counsellor at any time.

The intention of this tutor-counselling effort at the beginning of a students course is to encourage learners to become skilled in group discussion and become relatively independent during the remaining years of their study, when the number of tutorials decreases. Students still keep their first year tutor-counsellor for any counselling and other study advice as they progress to higher level courses.

In addition to the formally arranged tutorial counselling sessions, a system exists to encourage and facilitate the formation of 'self-help' study groups, meeting in people's homes, pubs, places of work and so on. Students at all levels have the opportunity to be put in contact with others studying the same course and living in their locality.

Whilst studying for a degree might not be considered by some to be the most appropriate type of learning for many unemployed adults (although it must be remembered that significant numbers of Open University graduates have had no previous educational qualifications), this particular system of counselling, tutoring and self-help study groups has much to offer as a model for groups of unemployed adults engaged in any distance learning.

The Open University is not only involved with degree courses. Large continuing and community

Distance Teaching and Self-Paced Learning

education programmes include short courses and packs of learning materials intended for study at other than degree level. The courses in Community Education do not have formal tutorial support but are promoted for use by groups coordinated by volunteers. Materials are used in a variety of ways designed to suit the needs of participants. Each course includes group study notes giving hints for activities and advice on how to organise a group. It is not assumed that a coordinator is necessarily a professional teacher.

Volunteers range from members of organisations such as Friends of the Earth to consumer groups and play groups to social workers and other carers. The Health Education Council, having commissioned the production of learning materials, now has a sponsored place scheme for those who are disadvantaged.

Some courses have a programme including radio and television and various assessments. Other courses are packages of learning materials in various forms to be used as convenient. The intervention and guidance of an experienced learner will help others to whom this form of study is unfamiliar.

Linden West in his comments on the MSC's Adult Training Strategy[11] argues for resources to be channelled to allow the exploration of possibilities for voluntary and/or community work on a more extensive scale than previously envisaged. He points to the experience of using volunteers in the adult literacy campaign and concludes that volunteers could be much more involved with the learning of unemployed people. They themselves could then act as voluntary tutors or co-ordinators of study groups, whether these involve others like themselves or those differently placed.

It is possible for learning materials to be used to benefit both the individual and the community as a whole. The following example, undertaken by Helen Munroe in Glasgow, could serve as a model for work with unemployed adults.

The project was designed to bridge the gap between the traditional approach to adult education - '"Evening classes" whether in politics or keep-fit, creative writing or yoga'[12] and the more radical view that sees all community activity as education. For the people in certain working class areas of Glasgow, the traditional offerings of adult

Distance Teaching and Self-Paced Learning

education, even when offered free, fail to get support. At the same time, relatively few people are involved in community action which might give them learning experiences. Even for those who are involved, Munroe argues, this kind of activity is educative rather than educational. They are educative in that the experiences are of a one-off nature rather than educational in the sense that a course of learning takes place which effects a change within the individual.

Munroe reports on the use of Open University short courses with women in deprived areas of Glasgow. The project began with discussions in the parents' room of a local nursery school. The discussions centred on the women's families, their men, children and homes, but with little direct interest in community affairs, the feeling being that individuals had no influence over these. The decision to use the Open University course 'The Pre-School Child' seemed relevant to these women's needs. The course is produced in an attractive magazine format with four linked television programmes and is essentially activity based. There are four optional assignments with multiple choice questions leading to a certificate of course completion.

There were fears that a 'course', particularly one produced by a university would be offputting to many of these women with no previous post-school educational experience. Munroe says, '...many adult educators are guilty of underestimating the potential in deprived communities. They are guilty of offering a deprived - and therefore depriving - curriculum e.g. "they'll not come to anything academic so we'll just give them sewing and keep-fit"'.[13] The support of the group leader is important in overcoming initial barriers and the fears turned out to be unfounded.

The Pre-School Child course as well as two other parenting and one health course have, since 1979, been used with about 35 groups in deprived areas all over Glasgow. The courses have been used in a flexible way, for instance, taking longer than the 10 weeks allocated by the University, doing the assignments as a group effort, and encouraging small self-help groups. Meetings take place in a variety of settings - nursery schools, playgroups, community flats, health centres. A woman with reading difficulties was helped with reading the course

Distance Teaching and Self-Paced Learning

texts but completed the activities herself, joining in the discussions with others as an equal partner.

There are many valuable outcomes from doing a course in this way. Firstly, there are the knowlege and understanding which comes from the content of the course itself. Secondly, this new understanding is transferred into the home situation of the women and their relationships with their children and families. Thirdly, there is the knowledge, gained mainly from the group discussions, that members are not unique in their problems. Fourthly, 'for some women, the course seemed to act as a launching pad for their talents, their confidence was boosted and they began to take part in community affairs - one became a schools' council representative; another a playgroup area organiser; two now run their own Open University groups; another is the secretary of a tenants' co-operative and several have continued in adult and further education courses with a view to professional training.'[14]

Other important aspects of these initiatives are that the professionals (teachers, health visitors, community workers, adult education workers) who have been involved in leading these groups say how much they have learnt in the process. Good adult education is teaching on equal terms and learning should be a co-operative and not hierarchical activity. Helen Munroe concludes,

> It seems that a relatively traditional approach to adult education ie a course, combined with a more radical community-based, co-operative style of learning can attract a new clientele (previously non-participants) and can have benefits for both individuals and the community as a whole. These courses would never have continued to be used and to expand if they did not appeal to people. They appeal because they deal with what are important topics in many people's lives - children. These courses begin "where people are" and then the scope can be widened.[15]

COLLABORATION

The example just described is one in which the course was a product of more than one institution. The creation of the learning materials involved the

Distance Teaching and Self-Paced Learning

university with the Health Education Council and the Scottish Health Education Council. The delivery and interpretation brought in the community education department. The benefits available to course participants were clearly enhanced by this collaboration at all stages.

The broadcasting media can play an important role in open learning systems. For example educational broadcasting for children and adults is well established and many correspondence courses have television and radio elements. There are good arguments that learning packages benefit from being 'media led'. Charnley et al report that local radio may attract to study many who do not normally participate in adult education classes because, 'there seems general agreement about television and radio being the sparking plug in any multi-media package'.[16]

The use of television and radio learning packages has advantages and disadvantages. Some argue that they add interest and can illustrate certain aspects of a course more effectively than print. They also act as 'pacers' encouraging students to keep up with their studies, in order to be at the right point to obtain maximum benefit from the broadcast. Others say that broadcasts constrain the flexibility with which the materials can be used. They impose a restricting time structure on the study. Obviously, this becomes less of a problem where broadcasts are replaced by recordings sent through the post.

When broadcasting elements are used within learning packages, three problems need to be faced in design and delivery. Firstly, the expectations of broadcasters may differ significantly from those of the educators. What is good television is not necessarily good education. Secondly, the different lead times required to prepare the varied components can lead to problems of integration of the parts into the whole. Thirdly, the broadcasting schedules may be inappropriate and inconvenient for an audience which is not very highly motivated. Late night timings will be impossible for groups, day time broadcasts may reinforce feelings of isolation and being different. These attitudes need to be recognised in any learning programme which includes a broadcasting element.

Distance Teaching and Self-Paced Learning

LESSONS FOR PROVIDING LEARNING EXPERIENCES FOR UNEMPLOYED ADULTS

Distance teaching and open learning systems such as those described above have much to recommend themselves in relation to learning related to unemployed adults. The range of distance learning materials available from any source is such that groups based on the study of these could be formed in any appropriate place - unemployment or community centres, social clubs, people's homes or wherever.

With some collaboration between different government departments, facilities could be found for adult education staff to form study groups within unemployment benefit offices and job centres - places which unemployed people regularly visit. Through this medium, arrangements could be made for unemployed people either to register for relevant qualifications, or be provided with packs of materials on which they can base home learning and study group discussion. They then have the advantage of continuity of study in their own home with the support of a study group, with an experienced though not necessarily specialist co-ordinator.

In this way, control of the learning experience remains with the learner, whilst, at the same time, learners have the opportunity of testing their knowledge and ideas against those of others in similar situations. Out of the group interaction can arise strategies for action - action which could improve the situation of individuals in the group and others. What is more, not only the mode but the content of study can be chosen to interweave with participants' everyday needs.

Munroe's work with women clearly showed how education which related to everyday problems could be successful. In her case the problems were related to children. It is not difficult to see how courses on welfare, housing, new business or alternative living could relate to a large number of unemployed people and could, in principle, be of great benefit to them.

For example, access to open learning materials based on running small co-operative businesses would have been relevant to the members of MEP at Sheffield. Study group discussions, at lunch time perhaps, would relate directly and at appropriate times, to the work of the members. In another case, a group of unemployed people concerned with

Distance Teaching and Self-Paced Learning

facilities in their local community or town, could base their learning, and subsequent action, on a course about local government and the services it provides.

Another group might use materials on welfare benefits which could lead to enlarged understanding of the social security system as a whole, its economic and ideological base. Study, in this case, can be intermingled with taking action to improve the situation both of those participating and of others. This action would be based on a deeper understanding of what is happening and how it might be influenced.

There is little purpose served by arguing that such courses as suggested in these examples are available already in various places throughout the country. Provision is patchy, learning is often divorced from action and the political dimension underplayed, avoided or ignored. In addition, it is clear that the majority of unemployed adults, indeed the majority of adults, do not participate in any education provided by Type I or Type II organisations at all. Opportunities to extend participation must be taken if education is to have a meaningful function.

NOTES

1. See Lindsay Martin, REPLAN and the Future of Adult Education, Occasional Publication No. 5, National Association of Educational Guidance Services, (1985), p.4

2. Linden West, 'A Response to the MSC's "Towards an Adult Training Strategy - A Discussion Paper", April 1983', Appendix One to Adult Education and Unemployed People, report of a workshop held on 14th May, 1983, WEA Berks Bucks & Oxon

3. Advisory Council for Adult and Continuing Education, Distance Learning and Adult Students, ACACE, Leicester, (1983), p.3

4. A.H. Charnley, M. Osborn and A.Withnall, Review of Existing Research in Adult and Continuing Education Volume IV, Open Learning and Distance Education, National Institute of Adult Continuing Education (England and Wales), (1981), p.2

5. K. Scales, 'A Typology Applied to Distance Education in British Columbia', Lifelong Learning, (November 1983)

6. Op.cit. see p.42

7. Ibid. see p.45
8. Ibid.
9. West, op.cit.
10. Charnley et al. op. cit.
11. West, op. cit.
12. Helen Munroe, 'Does Adult Education Have a Role in Community Education?', <u>Strathclyde Studies in Community Education</u> Volume 2, p.25
13. Ibid. p.29
14. Ibid. p.30
15. Ibid. pp31-32
16. Charnley, op. cit. p.33

Chapter Eight

A MODEL FOR DISTANCE LEARNING PROVISION FOR UNEMPLOYED ADULTS

Chapter seven established some principles which could be used as a basis for the development of effective distance learning. In addition, the example of Helen Munroe's experiences showed how practical achievements could follow from the use of appropriate materials with participants who were motivated to learn through them. The motivation in Monroe's case stemmed from the problems of bringing up children. We now go on to address directly the question of reproducing this success in another context, that of unemployment.

The issue concerns the blending of two themes, distance learning and community education. The latter has been defined in various ways. For example, the Open University sees it in the following terms:

> Community Education is concerned with learning of individuals in, for example, their roles of parent, consumer, employee and citizen in the context of family, work place and community. Through a process of dialogue, it helps people as individual learners to be informed, to reflect on their experience, to become aware of alternatives, to decide what they want, and to take appropriate action to achieve it. Co-operation with others in the locality provides both support for learning and help in bringing about changes for the benefit of the community.

Model for Distance Learning Provision for Unemployed

> Community education cannot change society on its own but when and where changes are taking place it can facilitate, inform and enable participation and help people to take action to influence the direction of these changes. It is, therefore, an integral part of community development.[1]

The paper from which these quotations are taken stresses that community education should build on what already exists, 'through strengthening social networks, developing appropriate materials and encouraging individuals to draw on and value their experience'.[2] Emphasis is placed on collaboration with others in identifying learners' needs, planning and preparing materials, producing and using them as well as taking part in the evaluation process.

This particular perspective in its curriculum and teaching is similar to what Lovett[3] calls the community development/education model. The Open University model of community education, though not subscribing to the view of community education which believes that all experience is learning whether structured or not, does subscribe to a view of education as something which involves both formal and informal processes, whilst still relying on some underlying structuring of those processes. There is an overall emphasis on personal change with the assumption that this will give participants the skills, confidence and strength to work towards bringing about desirable social change.

Experience shows that distance learning and community education can be linked successfully. People who see much of current educational provision as irrelevant to their lives do, even so, want to learn. They will participate in learning if they can see direct links with improving their life chances and can retain control over their own learning. The examples of Open University courses in health and child development show this.

In these cases it was assumed that learners had particular motivation to learn about some quite specific issues. The commonality between the learners was perceived as being more significant than their individuality and course design could be related to this. In contrast, our arguments have tended to stress individual needs of unemployed adults. While they may be willing to come together to participate in joint learning activities, they

Model for Distance Learning Provision for Unemployed

each bring along a different set of problems and are seeking different outcomes. We shall now examine ways in which this problem may be overcome.

APPLYING THE MODEL TO UNEMPLOYED PEOPLE

During the twelve months from January 1983 to January 1984, one of the authors visited a wide range of people throughout the UK, whose interest was 'unemployment', either because they themselves were unemployed, or because they wanted to do something to help those who were. These people included members and co-ordinators of unemployment centres, educationists in all the variety of sectors, trade unionists, church workers, local authority officials and elected members, supervisors and those working on government employment schemes, managers of private training agencies, those working in rehabilitation centres and so on.

Each contact was asked what type of educational provision was appropriate for adults who were unemployed. The responses indicated the need for flexible arrangements where learners could find out what their inclinations were, and follow them. Much of the information gained in this way, however, related to the content of what might be offered. This ranged from helping with the more practical aspects of being unemployed - obtaining benefits and coping financially - through taking the opportunity of time to develop interests and leisure pursuits to suggestions about dealing with issues related to unemployment itself and the system which produces and sustains it.

Some educationists were sceptical about whether a single programme could focus on more than a few things. Others had themselves devised programmes which were overwhelmingly based on classes and courses which they maintained met most of the perceived need. Yet others declared formal education to be a non-starter with the majority of the people who are unemployed, there being little experience of education on the part of these to encourage them into it now.

The most interesting feature of the responses was the very limited reference made by educators to the learning process. It could have been that they had considered this, but realised that they had little scope for changing the framework in which

Model for Distance Learning Provision for Unemployed

they operated. Issues of design of the learning process itself, control and monitoring of activities and the problem of introducing change were rarely discussed. Yet, some of the more innovative educational projects are those which directly address these issues. Alicia Bruce, reporting on several projects in Scotland, says:

> The success of such schemes is due not so much to a body of knowledge and skills, but rather to the style of delivery of the service: personal, informal, flexible, local and co-operative. ...These projects are developing models relevant to the unemployed, and others, by initiating learning groups in each community, tailored to the particular needs the applicants express.[4]

Putting together the results of these discussions, investigations and the Open University's experience, conclusions were reached regarding the nature of any provision of educational opportunities for unemployed adults. These were then related to the concept of a blend of distance learning and community education to produce a proposal for provision which would have the following objectives:

To enable unemployed people individually and in groups to:

(i) explore the characteristics of, and explanations for, unemployment in relation to their own experiences.
(ii) examine the practical, social and psychological effects of unemployment on themselves, their families and communities.
(iii) identify their own individual and/or group short and long-term objectives relative to the opportunities and constraints within their environment and the alternative courses of action open to them.
(iv) take appropriate action to achieve these objectives.

These are more specific expressions of the general aims presented in Chapter three. They require that there needs to be incorporated into any learning experience the opportunity for learners to do at least two things. One is to gain process skills such

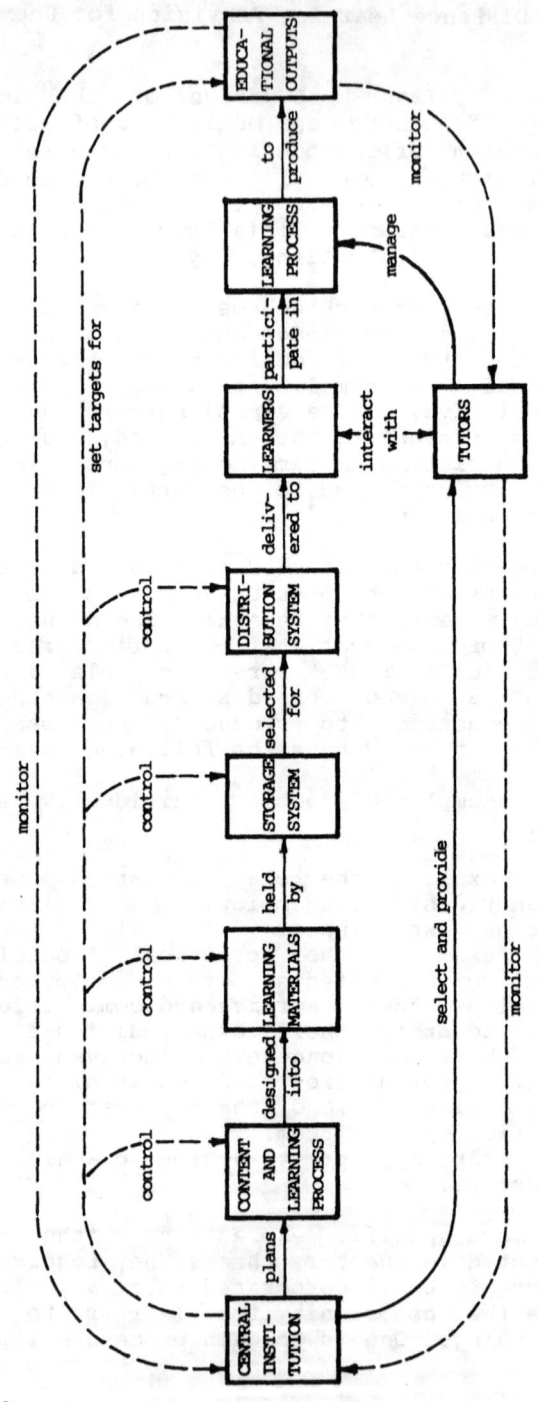

Figure 8.1: Centralised Distance Learning System

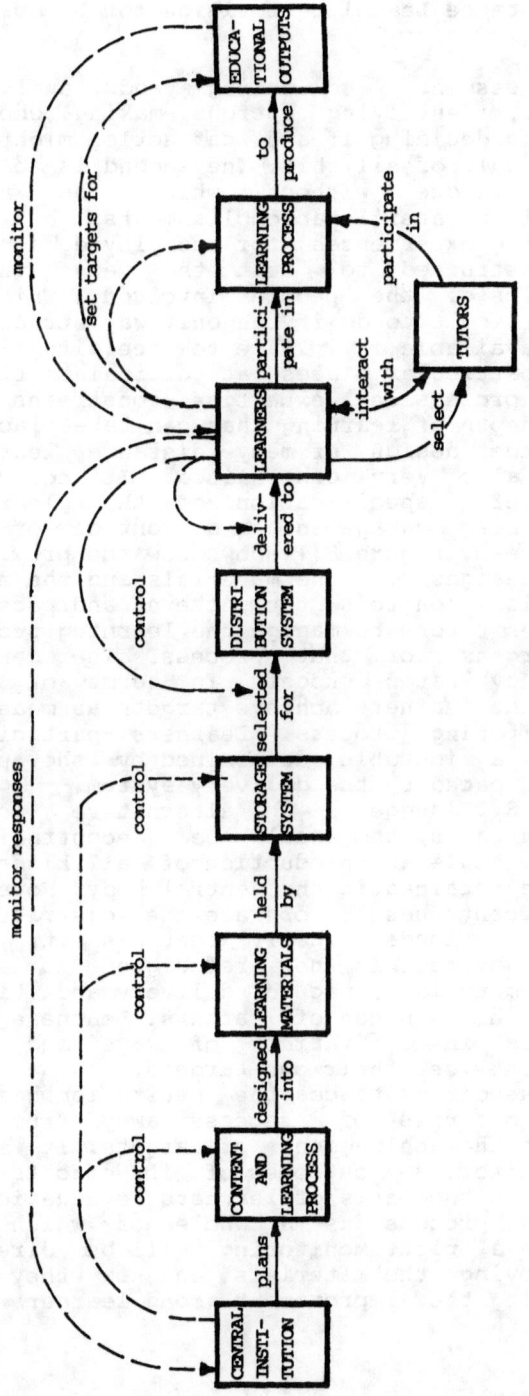

Figure 8.2: Decentralised Distance Learning System

as self-assessment, collecting and analysing relevant data, identifying options, making choices among them and deciding if and what action might be taken as a result of all this. The second is to gain essential knowledge without which the above processes will be sterile accomplishments.

Learning experiences for unemployed adults, must be constructed to suit the very varied characteristics of the people involved. This is extremely difficult to do if the only way structured learning is available is in face to face situations, located in particular places at particular times. Reliance on professional expertise constrains the breadth and depth of learning that can take place.

Yet the design of many distance learning systems is also very centralised. It not only includes careful specification of the learning content but also management and control of the learning process. Figure 8.1 shows how the providing institution designs both the materials and the means of distribution, controls the pattern and pace of delivery, uses tutors to manage the learning process and sets targets for that process. The central institution evaluates success in terms of how effectively the learners achieve targets as measured by the monitoring process. Learners participate according to a timetable determined by the plan, motivated and paced by the delivery system.

Figure 8.2 suggests an alternative model, whereby such a system could be decentralised. Economies of scale in production of all kinds of materials are retained in the central body. However, although it continues to operate the distribution system, it no longer wholly controls it. The distribution system is now redesigned to allow selection of materials, pace of delivery and timing of use to be in the hands of learners. Learners use the materials in a variety of ways and, in particular, they set their own targets.

In these circumstances the institution has to change its measures of success away from an evaluation of the achievement of targets. It still needs to monitor the outcomes of its efforts but this will be on the basis of learners' evaluation of the learning process as a whole of which the materials are a part. Monitoring will be directed towards improving the materials and how they are used. Measuring the improvement among learners now

Model for Distance Learning Provision for Unemployed

becomes solely the concern of the learners themselves.

The roles of tutors, or facilitators, change between the two models. In Figure 8.1 the tutor is the local extension of the central institution. In Figure 8.2 the tutor may be used by learners in a variety of ways and would have a valuable role in development of the learning process itself. Thus learners are wholly involved in setting their own targets, maintaining control over their own learning processes and assessing their own achievements. They are supported by a mixture of learning materials and human resources.

A PRACTICAL EXAMPLE

The course 'Action Planning' has been developed at the Open University with these ideas in mind. It consists of a set of structured learning materials designed to meet the needs of unemployed adults. The complete pack has been produced, with funding from the DES and MSC, as part of the University's Community Education programme and has the following aims:

To help unemployed adults to:
    (a) tackle the immediate practical problems associated with being unemployed.
    (b) assess their interests, achievements, skills and potential.
    (c) explore options open to them in the future.
    (d) choose which options to pursue, draw up and implement appropriate action plans.

The core of the learning materials is fifty, free standing, four page topic leaflets designed to structure the learning process for the user. This means that, in contrast to straightforward information giving resource materials, these leaflets include a range of teaching devices - simple checklists, questionnaires, projective exercises, analysis of case studies, value clarification, multi-dimensional rating, practical activities, observations and simulated role play - with feedback built in. This means that 'learners can compare their experiences and views with those of others and can see where they stand within a framework of possibilities'.[5]

Model for Distance Learning Provision for Unemployed

The leaflets are organised around eight themes under the overall title of 'In and Out of Unemployment'. Three of the themes emphasise process skills, focusing on different aspects of self-assessment rather more than taking action. These are called 'Self-Assessment', 'Survival' and 'Social Support'. The other five, whilst not neglecting entirely the development of process skills, concentrate more on knowledge required and how to use it in order to take action regarding chosen options. They are 'Group Initiatives', 'Work in Your Life', 'Personal Development', 'Special Groups', and 'Action Planning'.

The first three themes, through their emphasis on process skills, are aimed at achieving the first three of the objectives set out in the previous section. They take learners through a process which helps them to decide on and plan their own strategies for achieving short term aims - perhaps related to coping with immediate problems - as well as choosing options for taking appropriate longer term action. The materials are designed so that learners, starting from their own life experiences, react to them in ways best suited to their own individual, family and wider community and societal needs.

The themes 'Group Initiatives', 'Work in Your Life' and 'Personal Development', as their titles suggest are more action orientated. Varied in their content, they concentrate on helping learners explore a number of options for action relevant to their individual and collective needs. More directional than the first three themes, they relate to the fourth objective of choosing options to pursue.

'Special Groups' as a theme is rather different. It focuses on the needs of those groups of unemployed people who might be considered particularly disadvantaged when it comes to employment and the labour market. Finally, the theme 'Action Planning' aims to help the learner bring together learning and action. Drawing on the options identified in other themes, it enables a summary of learning to be made and definite plans for action to be drawn up.

It is clear that the action orientated themes cannot include everything that an unemployed individual or group might want to do. Thus if learners need knowledge and the means to take action

Model for Distance Learning Provision for Unemployed

not provided for in the materials, they are referred to other forms of provision and sources of information.

The form of the learning materials reflects the principles of user control while at the same time recognising that central production does result in low costs. The written materials are in leaflet form, far less aggregated than is normal in distance learning packages. Not only does this allow simple modification but it assists the learner in recognising that part of the process is choosing a way through a number of activities or themes. The group, or individual, is engaged in a structured learning experience yet, in as much as the structure is built from a number of small units, embellished and added to at will, it is chosen by the learner rather than the provider. The materials can, therefore, act as a springboard from which learners may 'take off' in any direction.

Audio recordings of other unemployed people's experiences and illustrations of the written materials enable the isolated learner to link with the reactions of others. Though currently not part of the course because of cost constraints, video materials, important in affective learning, would motivate learners to take action themselves when they see what others have done.

As Figure 8.2 proposes, the delivery system is under the control of the learner. Material is available easily and at any time to unemployed individuals or institutions and organisations whose interests are in helping those who are unemployed. These range from drop-in centres to colleges.

Support for learners is a critical issue. Given easy access to such a range of self-contained materials, isolated learners may come to regard them as simply information leaflets which, although attractive, are basically to be read. In such circumstances the learner may never develop the process skills which are so crucial to successful action. The learner will also not gain one of the important elements of the design, that of overcoming isolation. Learner support systems, therefore, seek to maximise the effective use of the materials. This argues for a group system similar to that built up by Helen Munroe and described in Chapter seven.

The course uses two means for the development of groups. One is the use of existing educational structures, including professional tutors. The other

Model for Distance Learning Provision for Unemployed

is the development of new self-help learning groups outside existing frameworks. Thus, the written materials include notes which give advice and suggestions on how to initiate and organise informal learning groups. These are based on the principle that any individual learner can act as a co-ordinator of, and facilitator of learning in groups.

One drawback of making such learning materials available through existing educational institutions may be that one form of central control is replaced by another. It is impossible to prevent this. However, the fact that materials exist independently of the institution, and those teaching in it, allows learners to maintain control over their own learning. In addition, particular attention is paid by the Open University to observing and evaluating the use of the materials in group settings, with a view to advising on the most effective ways of using the materials in line with the principle of learner control.

TESTING THE MODEL

In Chapter two the conclusion was reached that any educational provision for unemployed adults should satisfy certain general aims. In addition, Chapter five put forward some educational perspectives which were considered relevant to the learning needs of those who are unemployed. It is pertinent now to consider how far the model described in this Chapter goes in achieving the aims and how it relates to the redefinition of education for unemployed adults made in chapter five. The first general aim is:

> Any educational provision for unemployed adults should take into account the different assumptions about the nature of unemployment and therefore the possible solutions.

The learning materials element of the model should, in particular, allow for achievement of this aim. The use of learning materials, in theory, allows an infinite variety and range of issues to be discussed. In practice, these are limited by the availability of resources, although it is probable that a wider range of issues could be addressed than

Model for Distance Learning Provision for Unemployed

can be dealt with within a conventional course. This allows for greater freedom of choice.

More importantly, the process orientated 'taking stock' themes are firmly based on learning through people's own experiences and perceptions. Thus, through carrying out a process of self-assessment, identifying relevant issues and options and considering what choices can be made, learners of necessity need to reflect on a number of perspectives on the problem of unemployment and the effects of it upon their lives.

It is also expected that group discussions based on individual experiences of unemployment and opinions about its causes and consquences will 'force' learners to consider views other than their own. The choice of allegiance to a particular perspective, however, remains their own. This will then manifest itself in how they choose the particular set of 'solutions' which seem relevant to them - which directions they want to go in.

There is a possible drawback. The central institution may wish to address a wide range of assumptions and solutions yet it will have to select from amongst these. This selection will be influenced by values both within the institution and elsewhere, particularly among providers of funds.

Seen in isolation, then, the more successful a distance learning system becomes, the more serious this problem becomes. If it replaces existing provision by attracting learners away from it then a more centralised system is the result. On the other hand, if it generates 'new' learners who are then encouraged to participate in other provision, only good can follow.

The second and third general aims were that:

> It should reflect the needs which are common to the majority of unemployed people as evidenced by the effects that unemployment has on them.
>
> There should be an appreciation that unemployed people are individuals who react to their situation in ways specific to them, their families and communities.

These aims may appear contradictory in their emphasis on common needs whilst at the same time implying that the individuals concerned are unique. Achievement of them both seems to imply some strict

Model for Distance Learning Provision for Unemployed

apportionment of what are 'common' needs compared to 'individualistic' needs. This is not so.

The argument used to support achievement of the first aim, applies also to these two aims. Thus, the emphasis on process - building on personal experiences, comparing and contrasting these with those of other people - implies of necessity a reflection of personal experience, but also setting these in the context of conclusions about the experiences of the majority of other unemployed people. Through the imposition of different learning structures and sequences of activities upon the materials, a number of approaches can be taken. Two are relevant here.

The first is that the learner may be asked to examine personal, individual experience. This is then compared and contrasted with the experiences (based on the research evidence available) of other unemployed people. The second approach, which does not preclude or compete with the first approach, analyses a situation at the 'macro' level, then asks the learner to position him/herself within a framework of what is common to most unemployed people. This approach can be likened to looking at a map of a town and then finding the indicator which says, "You are here."

The result of either of these two approaches is to recognise the individual unique qualities of the learner whilst at the same time saying, in effect, 'You are not alone in all this.' The opportunity to make choices of options and to follow them via the action orientated themes, bears directly on the third aim in its situation specific focus.

The advantage of the flexibility of form of this provision is that it enables any part of the whole package to be used to support many different purposes. This is especially important in any redefinition of provision as discussed in Chapter five.

For instance, many parts of the materials will challenge the work ethic. The deliberate assumption that alternatives to unemployment are not necessarily conventional employment, and the varying directions which can be taken, guarantee this. In addition any piece of material, according to the issues it deals with, can be used to support incidental learning, learning for its own sake, or the 'need to know'. The last two mentioned require signposts to other provision outside the framework of the learning materials.

With regard to learning for capability, the inherent structure of learning materials such as these, (with their emphasis on the processes of collecting and analysing data, using this to make decisions about options and taking steps to act upon these decisions) of necessity requires the development of those skills which contribute to all round capability.

CONCLUSION

In presenting a flow model of a distance learning system it was possible to identify critical stages of the system which were under the control of the providing institution. In designing a structure which was more appropriate to the needs of unemployed adults it is necessary for the central body to cede some of its control and be prepared to operate in a less certain way.

Learners could take on responsibility for their learning objectives and the learning process. Tutors could take on more of the role of facilitators and could, in effect, be 'employed' by the group rather than provided by the central institution. In addition, carefully designed learning packages could be made available in such a way that selection and delivery were much more decentralised than is normally the case.

The 'Action Planning' course is an example of this provision. It presents learning materials whose quality benefits from the research and production resources of a large body. The learning process has developed from the traditions of the Open University although conventional timetables and centrally patterned course structures have been removed.

There has, therefore, been some progress towards meeting the needs of learners. But it may not have gone far enough. The inclusion of a wide range of views on the economic and political basis of unemployment remains merely a possibility. In practice the material is constrained by budgets and time and the range of issues covered reflects both the values and the research work of the production team as well as the views of the sponsoring authorities.

Model for Distance Learning Provision for Unemployed

It could be argued that, if it is possible to decentralise the control of the learning process, then the choice of content could also be decentralised. Rather than the tyranny of one central body, justified by economies of scale, producing huge quantities of learning materials, it may be possible to have a different means of control.

Firstly, the central body could be controlled by representatives of the learners themselves. If production economies of scale are so important as to require just one central body, then this approach, modelled on the increased numbers of student governors in colleges, could ensure that the learners receive what they want. Whether effective control could be achieved at such remote range is, of course, a serious difficulty.

A second approach, again recognising production efficiency, would allow unemployed people and others access to the production system so that materials are produced both by insiders and outsiders.

A third view would separate the educational content of the material from its conversion into physical forms. The idea creation and production would take place separately in a similar way to a publisher producing an author's book.

Finally, as production methods alter to mean that optimum costs are reached at smaller outputs, it becomes more feasible to have several independent distance learning systems. Taken together, this pluralist group would go a long way to ensuring that a range of explanations and prognostications was available to each individual learner.

NOTES

1. 'Extract from the Final Report of the Interim Delegacy for Continuing Education Working Group on Community Education', Paper 1.1, July 1979, in <u>Community Education with the Open University, A collection of papers edited by Nick Farnes, Volume 2, 1979-1984</u>, Community Education, The Open University, Walton Hall, Milton Keynes, p.6
2. Ibid. p.7
3. Tom Lovett, Chris Clarke, and Avila Kilmurray, <u>Adult Education and Community Action</u>, Croom Helm, London, (1983), see pp.37-38
4. Alicia M.E. Bruce, 'Developing Alernative Educational Opportunities for Unemployed People', in

Model for Distance Learning Provision for Unemployed

Kate Vincent and Trevor Davis (eds) <u>Unemployment Strategies. A Search for a New Way Forward</u>, The Alternative Employment Group in Scotland, (1984), p.44

    5. N. C. Farnes, 'The Development of Parent Education Materials - The Van Leer Project', Paper 2.1, September 1981, in Farnes (ed) op.cit. p.40

Chapter Nine

THE FUTURE OF WORK AND THE FUTURE OF EDUCATION

FUTURE CHOICES

The future of education is bound up with the future of employment. The strength of this binding is a matter of debate. Education has always, in modern times, devoted much of its activity to preparing learners, or refreshing them, so that they can make effective workers. In Ralf Dahrendorf's phrase, education has been seen as producing 'spare parts for the economic machine'.[1] The question concerns how far education, both now and in the future, should be developed on this basis. Dahrendorf is clear. Education ought primarily to be a service to the individual, to enable people to become better people. It should be available as a matter of right all through life. In a future where the maintenance of liberty and the pursuit of quality of life are paramount, education based on responses to individual needs is able to counteract centralised, bureaucratic, oppressive forces which are typical of a more materialistic society.

Eric Schumacher[2] concentrates on the unseen inefficiencies of modern bureaucracies and casts education in a further role, additional to that of serving individual needs. Education should be a catalyst and facilitator for change. For Schumacher, the purpose of education is to gain an understanding of the present world, the world which we inhabit and within which we make our choices.

Futurologists such as these, together with Handy, Kelvin, Robertson and Watts, whom we discussed in Chapter two, base their views of the future not on extrapolation of trends but on responses to changes needed to solve the problems of

The Future of Work and the Future of Education

the present day. In some cases we are presented with a number of scenarios which might happen. In others we are persuaded as to what ought to happen. Dahrendorf is responding to personal experience of totalitarian regimes, Schumacher to bureaucracy. Not many clues are given as to how to reach the new future. Education is a possible vehicle yet it is so much a part of society that it cannot move outside of it. Socialisation and intellectual development take place as much outside the classroom as within it. Informal and incidental learning are so significant that a non-materialist, libertarian education could hardly be effective in a materialist, power orientated world.

Education cannot lead society to the promised land. There is no consensus as to where it is, how to get there or even whether we should go. By the same token, education should not prevent a survey of the route and the making of choices. We have agreed that an excessive proportion of post compulsory education provision is predicated upon one view of the future.

In contrast to those discussed above, this view is based on an extrapolation of current trends. The official view is that government, by judicious manipulation of the macroeconomic control levers available to it, can maintain a system whereby wealth can be reasonably shared and equity achieved. Intervention in markets to improve their efficiency eventually ensures that resources are used where they are most needed. Wealth and opportunities increase and unemployment falls. Yet, we have already shown how independent forecasts do not support the notion that unemployment will fall, given an extension of the current policies.

Of course, it is possible to restrict overtime, raise the school leaving age, lower the age of retirement by five years and so on. But these are coercive solutions. The social and psychological consequences of unemployment will not go away if they are transferred arbitrarily from one group to another. Many people would prefer to retire younger or leave school later; yet again many others would prefer paid employment rather than compulsory schooling or retirement.

The purpose of this book is not to show what the future will be like but rather that the future is very uncertain. It is most likely that high levels of unemployment, as currently defined, will

The Future of Work and the Future of Education

remain for the time being. Its burden will continue to be unevenly borne with a greater load being placed on those who live in northern cities, are unskilled and not so healthy. They will not be the inheritors of the new liberty. This is not 'the liberty of the poor man to dine at the Ritz',[3] but the freedom to choose among alternative ways of life. Liberty is not freedom to trample on one's neighbour but having access to choices, being able to explore the consequences of various courses of action and then being able to take opportunities as they arise.

In order to satisfy the needs of unemployed people, and, indeed, the needs of the whole society, education must adopt the central value of choice. We have shown that, currently, the dominant value of society is economic growth. Education provision for adults is thus based on development and maintenance of skills for current needs and also for stock. Economic growth is both stimulated and facilitated by the supply of appropriately trained workers. We have also shown the inherent weaknesses of this approach. Not only may much of this stock of skills never be needed, but the experience of learners is one of rising cynicism. The production of higher stocks becomes a victim of its own success as participants learn that their new skills are no more required than their old ones.

The case must not be overstated. The materialist would point to society's enjoyment of vacuum cleaners and videos, computers and cars, all produced in factories manned by an increasing proportion of technicians. The repair worker must also be well trained. The point is that the future will require rather less technicians than the present workforce has as automation increases, products become more reliable and service becomes self-service. For those who do not have paid employment, as currently defined, there need to be choices other than sitting and waiting for something to turn up. Indeed, the choice must include whether to participate in conventional employment or follow some viable alternative.

Education can both facilitate and be part of the choice. In order to do so there need to be changes at all levels from the content and process of learning to the structures of existing institutions and the creation of new ones.

The Future of Work and the Future of Education

THE FUTURE OF EDUCATION

A world which does not revolve around the idea of employment for the whole of one's life requires a different education provision. It should involve more than reading and writing and collecting certificates. It should encourage the development of the kinds of capabilities described in Chapter five. People will need practical skills and interpersonal skills, those required to work in the home and the community, and those which will enable them to get full benefit from leisure and to undertake self-organised work. Above all, people will need to be much more aware of, and in control of, what is happening to them, their communities and society.

This means the provision of more social and political education of a kind which is accessible to 'ordinary' people. It also implies exposing people to different political views and prejudices, to a variety of ideologies and theories about how society can be organised. In such an education system there would be roles for artists, writers and philosophers as well as social and natural scientists. The future of employment and unemployment would be an important and creative debate. The present fear of teaching which involves anything which can be labelled 'political' must be overcome. Learners should be treated as intelligent, responsible adults, able to form their own views and make decisions about their own lives.

There will, of course continue to be a requirement for education and training relevant to the needs of employment organisations. The further education sector, despite difficulties in knowing what employers want, remains able to carry out training for jobs. It would have to be changed in two ways. Firstly greater care would need to be exercised that the proposed jobs did exist. Secondly the training should be based on the whole year round working patterns of firms and other organisations, rather than the 36 week teaching year now used. Training should be available 'on tap' as it were, when and were it is needed so that trainees could move quickly into jobs. Employers will, however, have to take much more responsibility for training people they want to work for them. The private sector in the United Kingdom spent only 0.15% of turnover on training in 1984.[4] This represents only £200 per annum per employee. As Bryan Nicholson, MSC

The Future of Work and the Future of Education

chairman, said, 'it suggests that too many employers and line managers look on training as a cost to be minimised rather than an investment to be optimised'.[5]

The adult and continuing education sectors, freed also from their terms and classes, using peripatetic teachers, broadcasting, audio and video recordings, could expand significantly to fulfil the needs of adults for learning for its own sake, learning because of a 'need to know', and learning which leads to some form of creditation as demonstration of particular skills to defined standards. The present distinction, other than in Scotland, between adult and community education should disappear, and there should more involvement of learners themselves in teaching and passing on knowledge and skills.

This is particularly important for people whom we now call unemployed, but who hopefully, in the future, will not bear this stigmatising label. It is heartening, in this respect, to have some support for these suggestions from the teachers themselves. The National Association of Teachers in Further and Higher Education (NATFHE) and the Association of Adult and Continuing Education in a discussion paper on adult unemployment say,

> All too often it is assumed that the unemployed are unable to organise educational provision for themselves. There is no reason why unemployed adults should not be encouraged to take their own initiatives in organising their own provision. If necessary, development officers should be appointed by local education authorities to facilitate this.[6]

Open Learning
The potential of open learning has yet to be realised both for education for living and education for jobs. Allied with the adult and continuing education services, it is a powerful way of opening up access to all. NATFHE, whose main purpose as a trade union is to protect teachers' terms and conditions of employment, sees open learning as a healthy development. Thus,

> NATFHE recognises the potential of open learning in bringing training and educational

opportunities to large numbers[7] of people who would otherwise be denied them.

Bryan Nicholson, referred to above, praises what he calls the 'user-friendliness' of open learning.[8]

The potential of open learning incorporating distance teaching and self-paced learning has barely begun to be fulfilled. There is a number of institutions offering employment related courses through the Open Tech schemes. However, open learning should not simply mean increasing access in the way education is provided, but also moving to a situation where everyone has equal access to education beyond compulsory school leaving age. For instance the Open University is not 'open' simply because it uses distance teaching techniques. More important is the openness inherent in the policy of admitting applicants without any previous educational qualifications. Thus, one of its most important achievements has been to show that people with no previous educational qualifications can and do achieve degree level qualifications. This, combined with a policy of assisting low-income students with their fees, has enabled many adults to return to education, this time mainly in their own homes, who would previously be denied access.

The role of higher education

We have referred to cases of universities and polytechnics which have become involved in provision of education for unemployed people (e.g. Leeds University, the Open University and Wolverhampton Polytechnic), and, clearly, there are many courses relevant to a variety of employments. There is, however, a strong case to be made for a much expanded role for higher education in the future. A document on Britain's future, produced by NATFHE, devotes considerable space to discussion of future demand for higher education as a whole and the new pattern for higher education which it would like to see emerge. It is worth quoting some of the statements made.

> A well educated population is a key factor in the development and maintenance of a sophisticated and advanced economic and social system. This is true not only of education and training directly applicable to specific industries and jobs; the overall level of

The Future of Work and the Future of Education

> educational attainment has a clear relationship to the intellectually imaginative and creative potential of a nation's workforce.
>
> The nature of employment itself is already changing, and is likely to continue to change, probably at an accelerated pace and the need to adapt to occupational discontinuities of many kinds will be at a premium in the future.[9]

The final paragraph of the document says,

> The higher education system of the future will be much less tied to full-time attendance at institutions, taught courses of set durations, entry requirements or formal examinations. It will be a system which is accessible through a variety of media, capable of meeting the needs of individuals or small groups of students more readily and more flexibly, more able to cope with students with differing entry points and different needs in terms of time, mode and duration of study.[10]

This discussion of the expanded role for higher education concentrates on changes in process, yet unfortunately seeks to retain its justification within the maintenance of an imaginative and creative workforce. There is a danger here. In arguing for the removal of traditional structures and constraints on the learning process, NATFHE is using a justification that this would make education more appropriate for a particular type of future. In so doing it invites further inspection, a challenge to the whole of higher education as to whether it is suitable.

If some provision can be more tailored to needs, why not all? Liberal, libertarian and creative education may have been protected by the existing structures even though access has been restricted to a few. The proposed step away from education for its own sake can be retrogressive. It is possible to direct students to study electronics, spanish or business rather than industrial history, Latin or sociology. In circumstances where external criteria are readily accepted and many constraints removed, it becomes easier to do so.

The Future of Work and the Future of Education

Control

The danger of centralisation of control is the reason why our arguments have gone further than proposals for change in process and content. The case of distance learning identified the forces, based on scale economies, which tended to centralise control. The learner, faced with such an efficient teaching machine, would stand in danger of being overwhelmed by the message.

Similar arguments can be directed against colleges which are increasingly controlled by a limited number of suppliers of funds and examination boards. For example, the new General Certificate of Secondary Education will be managed by many fewer examination boards than hitherto. Colleges are controlled by education authorities and have as major stakeholders, the MSC and employers. Learners, particularly unemployed adults, have a very minor control function and remain in the role of clients who consume what is on offer. This is not an argument for more student governors or a return of some powers from central to local government. These changes may bring benefits, but they replace one controlling group with another. The client would not have more choices.

The key lies in decentralisation. What is required is a range of provision existing in different institutions to which a user has free access. It should not be a case of choosing between a local college and distance learning, a choice often constrained by personal and economic factors. There should be several colleges and several distance learning systems, each making available different learning experiences. They should not compete according to how efficiently they teach examination classes but on how they respond to individual needs. It is through pluralism that the centrality of the individual and the value of liberty can be recognised.

CONCLUSION

In this final chapter a picture of education provision in the future has begun to emerge. In a society where economic goals are moved from the centre of the stage and replaced by the pursuit of quality, equity and liberty, we must begin to think of a different education system. Legitimation based on the supply of skilled workers, together with control based on individual needs to improve job chances, would be replaced by a different philosophy. In such a future the stigma associated with unemployment disappears and education for unemployed adults is education for all.

So why concentrate on the adult unemployed as a group at all? In any future, unemployment becomes no longer a problem. Either it falls through rapid economic growth and society returns to business-as-usual, or people gradually develop coherent alternatives to the employment-unemployment divide.

Yet the problem for today's unemployed is that the future, or at least part of it, has arrived. The opportunities to exercise choice have not come along with the enforced idleness. They need to discover opportunities, open them up and take action to improve their lives. At the same time they need, and want, to survive and improve their chances.

An appropriately designed, flexible, pluralist education system is not only required in the future. Many people need it right now.

NOTES

1. Ralf Dahrendorf, *The New Liberty*, RKP, London, (1975)
2. Eric Schumacher, *Small is Beautiful*, Blond & Briggs, (1973)
3. Dahrendorf, op.cit.
4. 'Open Tech Open Day', *NATFHE Journal*, April 1985
5. Ibid. p.16
6. NATFHE/AACE, *Adult Unemployment, A Discussion Paper*, National Association of Teachers in Further and Higher Education, London, p.11
7. *Open Learning, A Policy Statement*, NATFHE, London, (1981), p.5
8. Op.cit.
9. *Britain's Future, The Economy and Higher Education*, NATFHE discussion document, National Association of Teachers in Further and Higher Education, (1984), p.10
10. Ibid. p.14

INDEX

Action Planning course 153
adult education 97,165
adult education centres 46
adult learning project 61,117-122
Advisory Council for Adult Continuing Education 41,49,88,135
Association of Adult and Continuing Education 166
attitudes towards unemployed people 37

Barnes, Jimmy 16
Belfast 11
Birmingham 52
Birmingham Unemployed Resource Network 87
black economy 8-11
Boyle, Connell 73
Bradshaw, Jonathan 10
Brighton 11
Bruce, Alicia 149
Bunker, Nigel 11-12

Cann, Roger 102-103,123
capability 104-105,159
centralisation 169
centres against unemployment 43

Charnley, A.H. 42,142
choice in education 164
Citizens Advice Bureau 4,53
collaboration 141
Colleges of Further Education 42,62,88
Community Colleges 94
community education 97, 100,106-107
Community Project Development Agencies 60
continuing education 165
correspondence courses 134
Cunningham, Lesley 121

Dahrendorf, Ralf 162
Daniel, W.W. 75-76
decentralisation 169
Department of Education and Science 56,64
Department of Health and Social Security 52,82
Dewberry, Chris 11-12
distance education 132
do-it-yourself 12-13

Edinburgh 59,117
education
    as social change 84
    definition 96
    employment related 70

Index

for capability
  100,104
for its own sake 168
for survival 79
general aims for
  unemployed people
  38,69,132,156
implications of
  different futures
  35-37
Educational Service
  Agencies 46
employability 80-81

financial survival 82
Frere, Paulo 61
Friends of the Earth 139
future choices 162
future scenarios 34-35,
  164-165,169

General Certificate of
  Education 169
Gershuny, Jonathan 36
Glasgow 139
Gravesend 51
Group Initiatives 154
Guthrie, Robin 4-5,13

Hakim, Catherine 21-22
Handy, Charles 7-8,12,
  33-34,162
Henry, Stuart 8,11
Her Majesty's Inspectors
  57,83
higher education 167
Hill, John 20
home and family 21
House of Lords Select
  Committee on
  Unemployment 5, 15
Hughes, John 78-85
Hull 54

In and Out of
  Unemployment 154
incidental learning 100,
  102,158
individualised study 136

infill schemes 47, 72
informal learning 163
Isle of Sheppey 13

Jahoda, Marie 11-17
James, Walter 99
job rehearsal 80

Kelvin, Peter 33,162
Kirkwood, Colin 59
Kirkwood, Gerry 120
Kumar, Krishan 95

Lancashire 51
learning 99
  for its own sake 100,
  158,166
Leicestershire 51
leisure 12-13
liberal education 100
Liverpool 52,124
Local Education
  Authorities 46,49,56,
  83,88
Londonderry 55,74
Lothian Regional Council
  117
Lovett, Tom 97,108,147

McDonald, Joan 46-49,58,
  61,71-72,74,80
Macarov, David 45
Manor Employment Project
  114-117,143
Manpower Services
  Commission 32, 41-42,
  46, 53, 56, 61-63,
  71, 98, 131
  Adult Training
  Strategy 77-79, 139
  Community Programme
  64, 73, 126
Martin, Lindsay 98,100
Merseyside Council for
  Voluntary Service
  124
Miles, Ian 11-12
Milton Keynes 58
Munday, John 74

Index

Munday, Sue 74
Munroe, Helen 139-141, 143, 143,155

National Association of Teachers in Further and Higher Education 73, 166-168
National Children's Bureau 22
National Extension College 134
National Institute of Adult Continuing Education 64,133
need to know, 158,166
The Network 124-128
Neuburger, Henry 28
Nicholson, Bryan 165-166
Northern Ireland 42, 88
Northern Ireland Council for Continuing Education 42, 50, 62, 74

O'Higgins, Michael 10
open learning 133, 142, 166
Open Tech 63,166
Open University 83, 88, 134,137,140,146,153, 167
    Community Education 40,48,146,153
    Continuing Education 134

Pahl, Ray 11-13
Participant Member Agencies 56
parents-school partnership 52
part-time employment 13
Percy, Keith 41,44
Personal Development 154
phase theories of unemployment 20
physical health 14-16

Policy Studies Institute 22
Polytechnics 46,55,81, 83,88,167
    Manchester 56
    Oxford 56
    South Bank 56
    Ulster 55
    Wolverhampton 52,167
Private Sector Agencies 64

raising the school leaving age 163
reflection on action 123
REPLAN 64,131
resource centres 43
Return and Learn 52
return to learning courses 58
Robertson, James 34,162
Royal Society of Arts 104

Schumacher, Eric 160
Scotland 149,166
Scottish Health Education Council 142
Second Chance Education 47, 80-81
Self-Assessment 152
Self-employment 35,77
Sheffield 61,143
Sinfield, Adrian 14,22
skills exchange 62,113 119
skills training 31,48
Social Support 154
Special Groups 154
study groups 137
suicide 15
Survival 154

Taylor, Robert 14
Technical and Vocational Education Initiative 31
Tit for Tat 118-124
training 31

173

Index

training 31
Training for Jobs 32,
    63,71,76
training for stock 32,76,110,
    164
Training Programme
    Contracting Agencies
    62
Traxler, John 99
Trew, Karen 11-12
The 21 hour rule 44-46,
    51,56,66,72
Tyrrell, R. 15

unemployed people as
    individuals 87
unemployment 9-23,27
    among the young
        19-20,27
    benefit 10
    centres 89,103
    and economic policy
        28
    long-term 18
    problem 28
    and social policy 28
    suggested solutions
        30-35
universities 81,83,88,
    94,167
    Bristol 53
    Durham 53, 80
    Hull 53
    Leeds 54,167
    Manchester 53
    The New University of
        Ulster 55
    Surrey 54
    The Universities
        Council for Adult
        and Continuing Educ-
        ation 53,54

Vulliamy, Daniel 54

Wallace, Claire 11
Warr, Peter 6,14,15,17,
    20
Watts, Tony 34,162

welfare rights 82
Wolfe, Ray 109
women 19,21,27,51,85,
    114,140
    work opportunities 63
    wider opportunities
        77
work 4
work ethic 94,110,158
Work in Your Life 154
work preparation courses
    63,77
work sharing 32,133
Workers Education
    Association 40,42,48,
    56,59,71,81,82,83,
    84,88,95

Yankelovich, Daniel 5
Young, Lord 28,78

For Product Safety Concerns and Information please contact our EU
representative GPSR@taylorandfrancis.com
Taylor & Francis Verlag GmbH, Kaufingerstraße 24, 80331 München, Germany

www.ingramcontent.com/pod-product-compliance
Lightning Source LLC
Chambersburg PA
CBHW051745230426
43670CB00012B/2171